Copyright © 2018 by PAUL F. BELARD

ALL RIGHTS RESERVED

ISBN: 978-0-9998939-4-4

Printed in the United States Of America
Linden Press
Greenlawn, New York

This book is one of a series of scholarly works which explore Elvis Presley's career and his impact on society here in the USA and abroad. It is a non-profit endeavor, and each book will be sold at cost.

First edition of 50 copies signed by the author

Cover design by Paul Bélard
Cover set up by Walter Sargent, sargentwebservices.com

Paul Bélard

ELVIS

September 1958

Linden Press
Greenlawn, New York

Preface

On the morning of September 22, 1958, a train arrived at the Army Terminal of the Brooklyn Navy Yard in New York City. Aboard was private Elvis Presley, along with a few hundred fellow GIs.

Elvis had been drafted in March 1958. Following six months of basic training, mostly in Texas, his unit was deployed to West Germany.

After giving press conferences in front of more reporters and photographers than an appearance from the then president of the United States, Dwight Eisenhower, would have assembled, Elvis embarked on a troop ship.

The USS Randall departed the Brooklyn Army Terminal at 2:00 PM. It would reach Bremerhaven, Germany, after nine days at sea, arriving in the early morning of October 1.

Opposite: Elvis during the Army press conference.

Monday 1 to Wednesday 17

Anticipating Elvis' departure for Germany, his manager made plans early in the month to schedule an event similar to the one arranged for his induction six months earlier. It would include press conferences, fans and reporters. Alluding to Elvis' induction, he wrote William Morris agent Harry Kalcheim: "I feel sure that you agree, it left a good taste and no circus flavor."

On Thursday 11, Elvis was assigned to the 3rd Armored Division based in Germany. His days were spent preparing for his forthcoming departure.

Vernon, Elvis' grandmother Minnie, and Lamar Fike would go to Germany, also accompanied by Red West whose stint with the Marines was just completed.

Pictures taken on September 12.

Thursday 18

Elvis spent his last night in Killeen with his father, Anita Wood, Eddie Fadal, some friends and several fan club presidents.

Above, from right: Frances Forbes, Red West, Lamar Fike, Junior Smith, Vernon, Elvis, Eddie Fadal, Earl Greenwood, two unidentified fans, Gene Smith, unidentified fan.

(DN4) KILLEEN, Tex., Sept 21--ELVIS AND GIRL FRIEND BEFORE DEPARTURE Pvt. Elvis Presley, accompanied by girl friend Anita Wood, prepares to drive from his home to join his Army outfit at Ft. Hood late Friday night. The rock 'n' roll singer is being transfered to Germany. Anita, who had been crying, refused to face the camera because she said she was red-eyed. Presley and his father rented the home here after the singer's mother died. His father plans to go to Germany to be near the son. (AP Wirephoto) (rbh10300str) 1958

Friday 19, Saturday 20, Sunday 21

Elvis left Fort Hood at 7:00 PM on Friday. The train was headed to New York where Elvis would embark to Germany on a ship docked at the Brooklyn Army Terminal.

On Sunday, somewhere during the trip, he for the first time met Charlie Hodge. They would start a friendship that would last all their lives.

On Friday, RCA released the album *King Creole*.

Above: Elvis leaving Fort Hood.
Opposite: Elvis and Anita on their way to Fort Hood. Caption and picture courtesy of Associated Press.

Elvis, holding his duffel bag, boards the train.

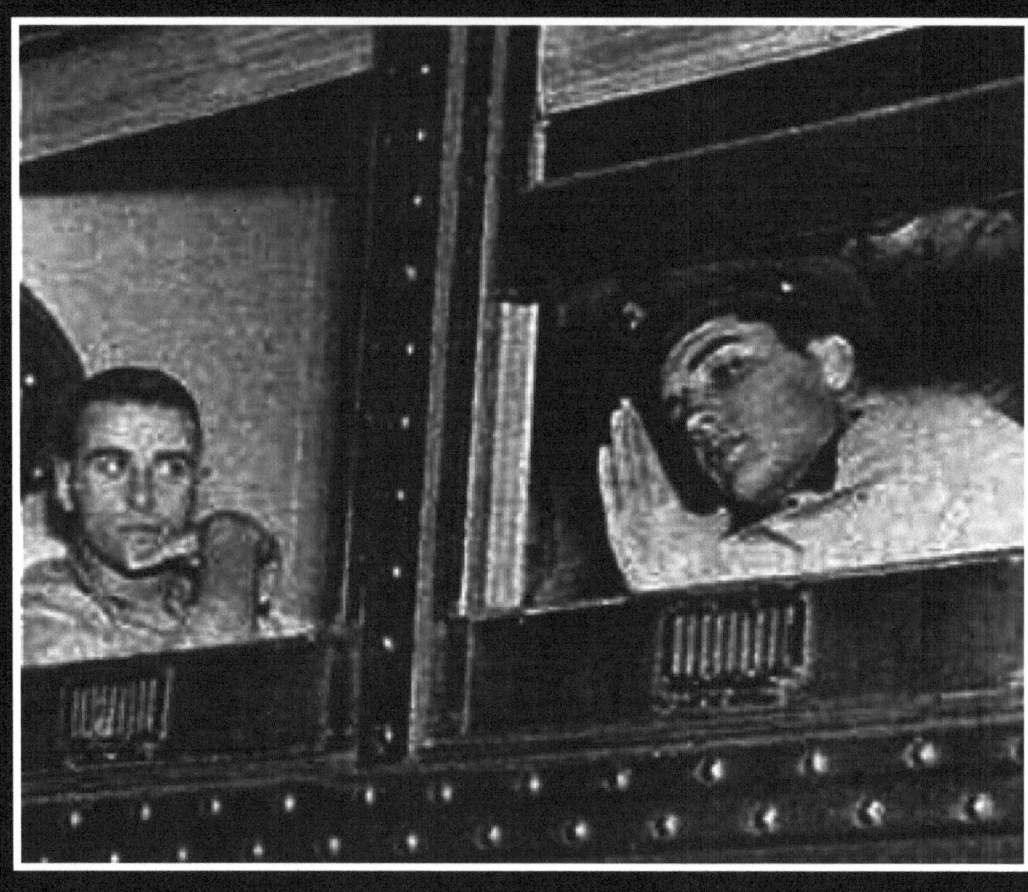

Elvis saying good-bye to some fans.

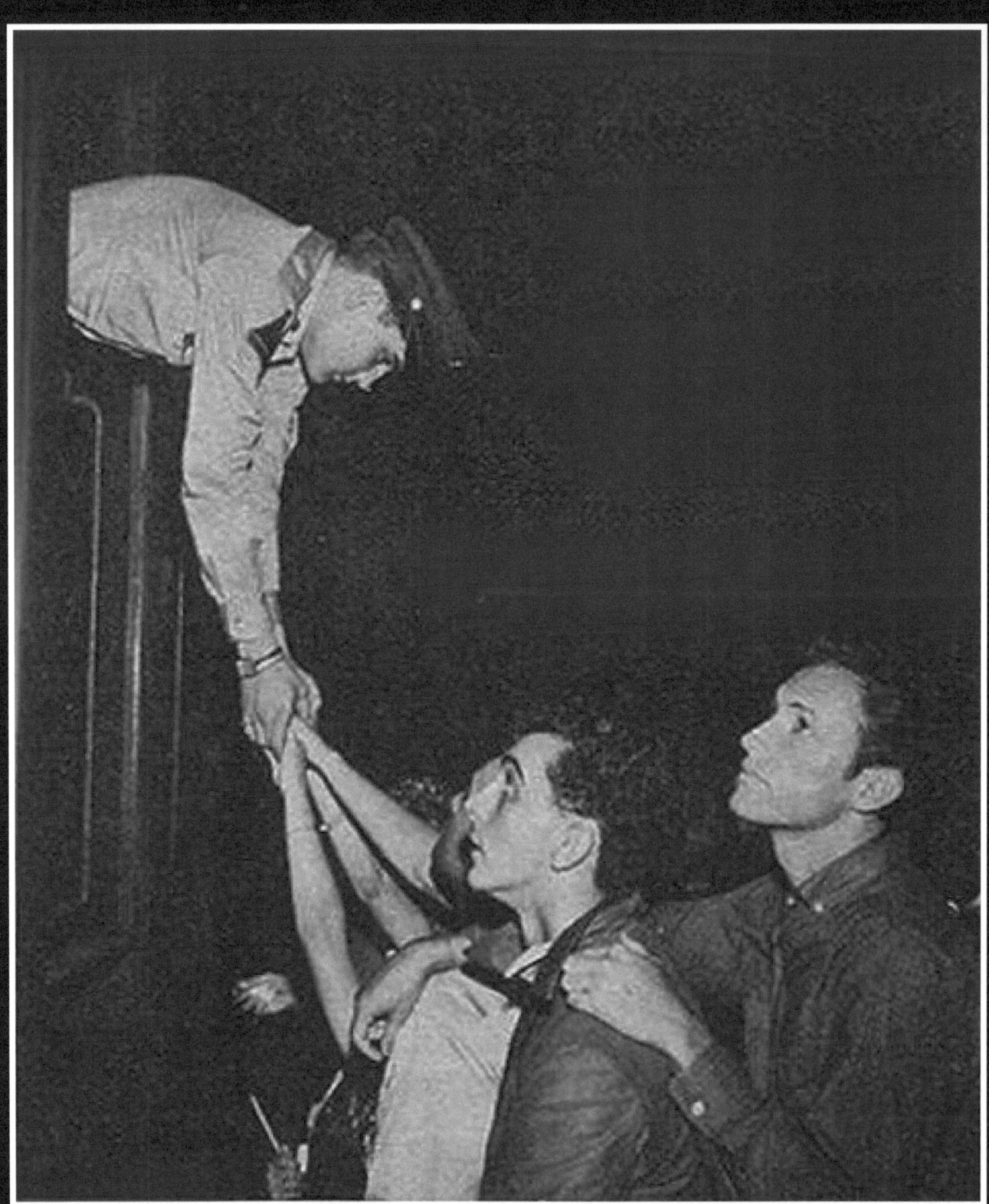

On Saturday 20, the train stopped for a while on a spur in Memphis. Elvis was not allowed to get off the train, but he came to the door. This is when he kissed Janie Wilbanks. A few months after, Ms. Wilbanks went to Grunewald in Germany, to visit her uncle, and stayed with Elvis for nearly a week around Christmas 1958

Above and opposite: Elvis shaking hands with Alan Fortas, Louis Harris, George Klein at the Memphis stop.

Opposite: Elvis kissing Janie Willbanks in Memphis during the stop. George Klein is to her right.

44 years later, girl who kissed Elvis celebrates his birthday

Ashley Elkins, *Daily Journal*, January 9, 2002.

Jane Wilbanks Gowen is now 62, a grandmother of four and wife of 29 years. On Tuesday, she remembered Elvis Presley as fondly as she did 44 years ago when she and the King courted in Germany.

"It was kind of Cinderella-ish," Gowen said.

Tuesday was the 67th birthday of the Elvis Presley. The singer died at age 42 in 1977.

Gowen dated Elvis for about 10 months while Presley, then 24, was stationed at a U.S. Army Base in Germany. She was 18. Gowen has scrapbooks of her teen-age years as a beauty queen and photos of her with Elvis in Germany and later at Graceland. A native of New Albany, Gowen first met Elvis as he was leaving Memphis on a train bound for Germany in 1958. She had actually encountered Elvis years before that occasion when both were teen-age contestants in a youth talent show at the Mid-South Fair.

Jane, whom Elvis called "Janie," said she and a group of her girlfriends went down to see the "Elvis Train," as it was called then, hoping to catch a glimpse of the superstar.

"He was in a part of the train where he could look out on the crowd," she said. "I had on this white leather coat and I had coal black eyes. I kind of stood out."

Gowen said Elvis has his friends help her on board the train.

"George Klein and another friend of his, Alan Fortas, helped me up the steps of the train he just started talking to me. I told him I was Jane Wilbanks of New Albany. He did kiss me," she said, pointing to a now famous black-and-white photograph which graced the covers of newspapers and magazines worldwide. "I have a wonderful memory of all of it. I thought to myself what an adventure."

Klein contacted her a few months later and said Elvis wanted her to write to him in Germany. When Gowen went to visit her uncle, Capt. J.P. Kirkland Jr., Elvis invited her to visit him at his hotel. She had her own room and her Christmas Eve date with Elvis was all very innocent, she said. It was a poignant holiday. His mother Gladys died in August and it was Elvis's first Christmas without his mother.

"He was sad and cried a lot, and I didn't know what to say," Gowen said. "Both of my parents were still living and it was hard for me to relate to that. He was still devastated."

The mood picked up for Elvis's birthday celebration on Jan. 8. Gowen was invited to help take part.

"They had a cake and he sang and played the piano," she said. "He played the piano much better than he did the guitar. I think he sang 'Happy Birthday Baby.' I gave him a royal blue velvet robe for his birthday."

After other guests departed, Elvis took Gowen to see a late-night movie. The two often talked about home and Mississippi, where Elvis had lived until age 13.

"He told me about growing up and how

they were so poor," she said. "We would talk about eating turnip greens and things like that. I think he liked talking with me because most of the time he had all these Hollywood starlets around. Of course I was from New Albany, which was only about 30 miles from Tupelo."

Gowen said she has resisted the temptation to capitalize on her courtship with Elvis four decades ago. She was interviewed by Peter Guralnick for his book "Last Train to Memphis" about Elvis's life. Gowen's courtship with Elvis is briefly mentioned.

"It was exciting and fun," Gowen said. "I did get to see him after he came home a few times. I went on to college and went on with my life as he went on with his life."

Gowen said she will never forget Elvis.

"It seemed like to me that when he walked into a room, he had an allure about him a charisma," she said. "I also noticed that even with a roomful of people, he seemed very lonely. He was just a famous man. But celebrities are real people, too. He had feelings, too."

Source: www.djournal.com via http://www.elvis-collectors.com

Above: The train arrives in the suburbs of New York City.

The *King Creole* album was shipped by RCA on September 19. Apart from "Steadfast, Loyal and True", all the songs had already been released on two extended plays and a single. In spite of this, the album sold a quarter of a million copies.

Eventually, It would be certified Gold on July 15, 1999 by the Recording Industry Association of America.

The album reached the number one position on the United Kingdom charts and number two on the *Billboard* Top Pop Albums charts.

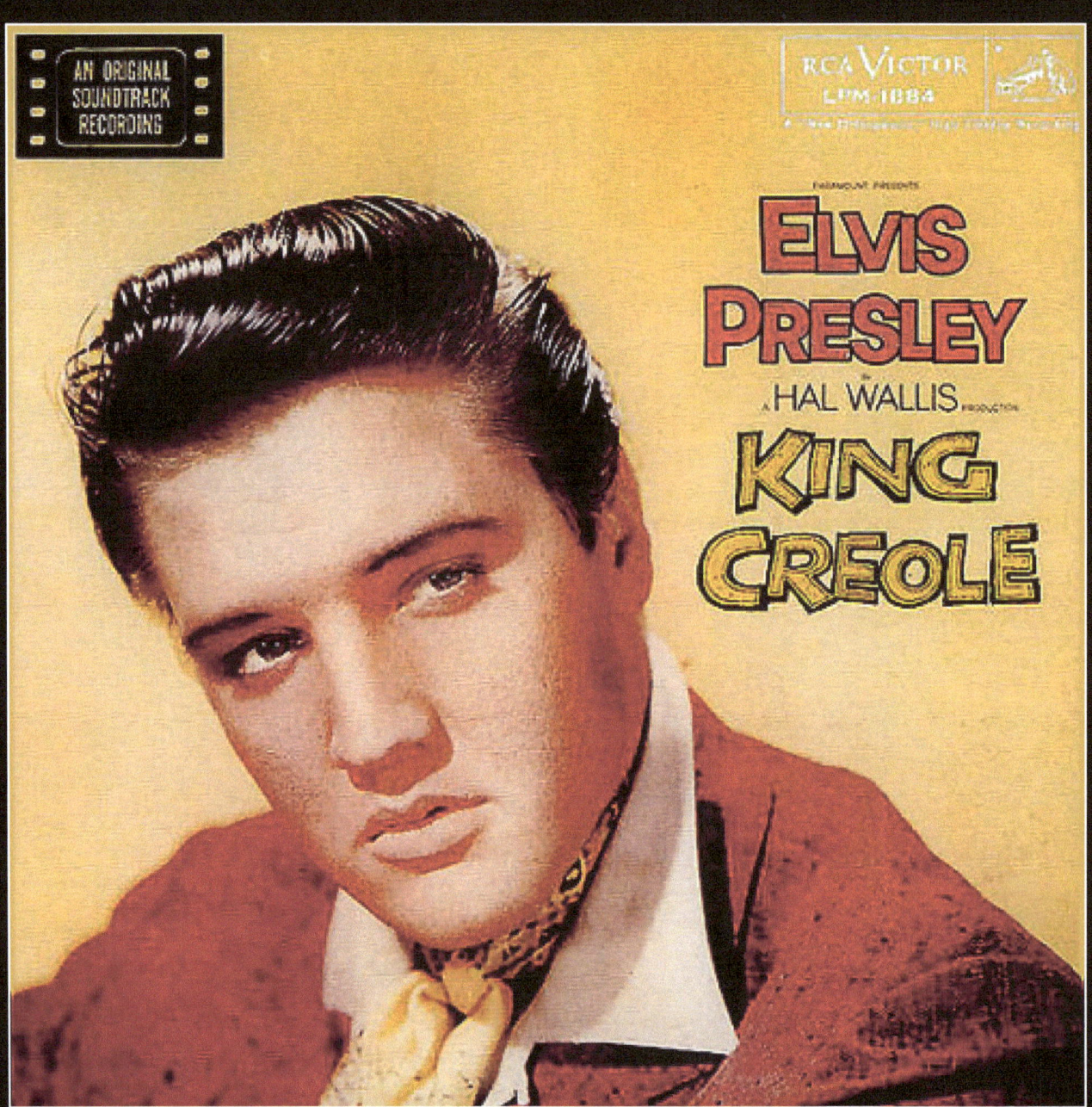

HEADQUARTERS
BROOKLYN ARMY TERMINAL
BROOKLYN 50, N.Y.

PUBLIC INFORMATION DIVISION
BROOKLYN ARMY TERMINAL
GEdney 9-5400, Ext. 2692

MEMORANDUM FOR THE PRESS

Private Elvis A. Presley, US 53310761, will depart from the Brooklyn Army Terminal today (Sept. 22) aboard the Navy transport, USS RANDALL. The ship will sail from Pier 4 at 2 pm with a total of 1771 officers, enlisted men and dependents, and is scheduled to arrive at Bremerhaven, Germany, on October 1st.

Private Presley was one of some 9,400 young soldiers being trained by the 2nd Armored (Iron Deuce) Division at Fort Hood, Texas, for duty with the 3rd Armored Division in Germany. More than 7,000 already have shipped to Europe.

In Private Presley's replacement packet are 1,360 troops from 16 different units of the Iron Deuce. They departed Fort Hood on four trains an hour apart on September 19, 1958. The first train carrying Private Presley departed at 7:30 PM, CST, and arrived at the Brooklyn Army Terminal this morning (Sept. 22) at approximately 9 am, EDST. The trains moved directly to the lower level of Pier 4, where the troops entrained and moved immediately aboard the transport.

Private Presley will come off the vessel at 10 am to attend a press conference which will be held in the Press Room on Pier 4, conducted by the Public Information Office of the Brooklyn Army Terminal

Army Press Memorandum about Elvis' departure to Germany.

On the 22nd, RCA shipped the extended play *Christmas With Elvis*. This is the second EP with four songs drawn from the *Elvis' Christmas Album* released in October 1957.

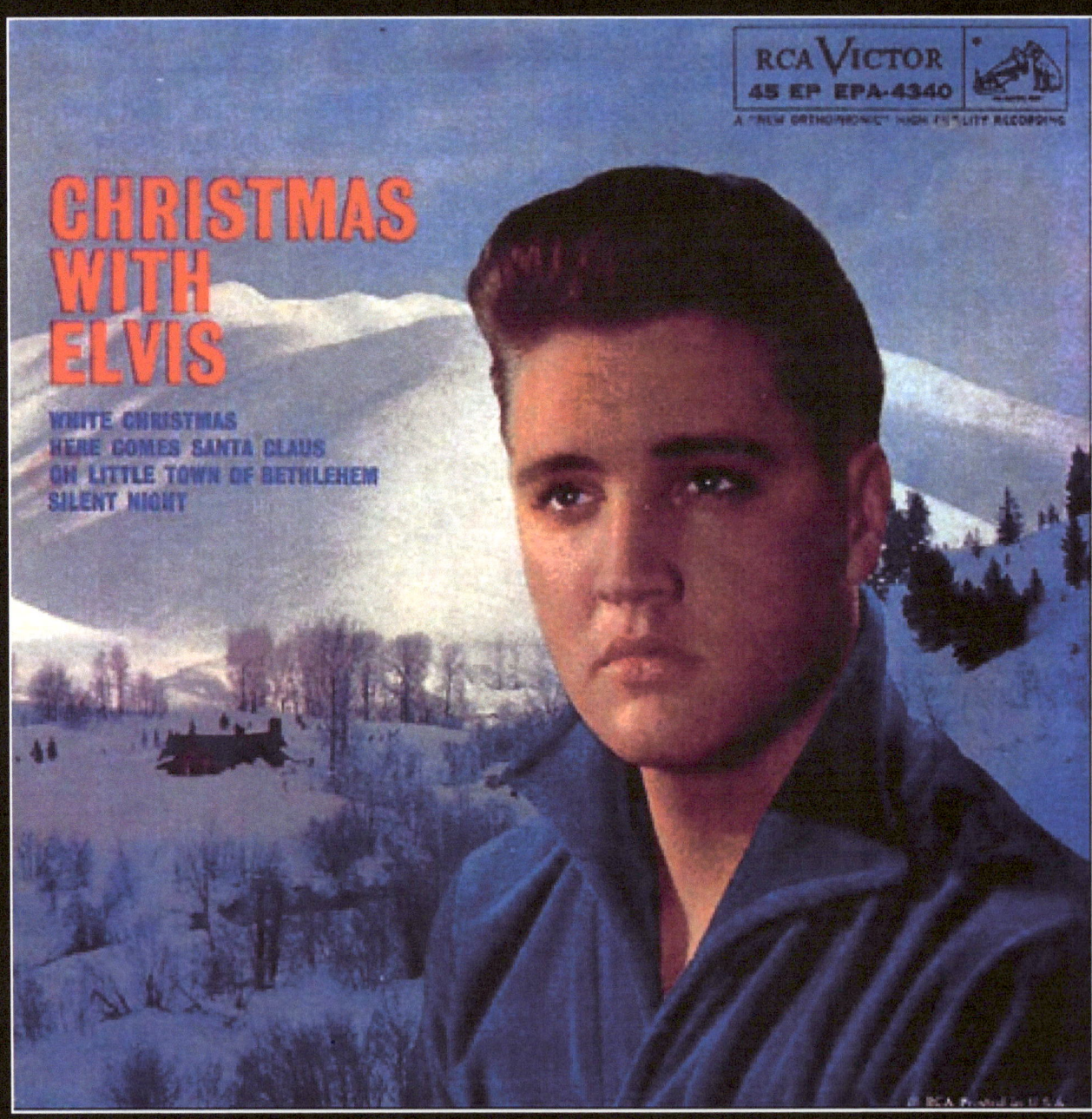

Monday 22

The train arrived at the Brooklyn Army Terminal at 9:00 AM. The troops embarked immediately onto the ship that would take them to Bremerhaven, Germany. Elvis came off the ship at 10:00 AM for a press conference. The ship departed a 2:00 PM.

Above: The troop train arrives at the Brooklyn Army Terminal. Photos in the following pages are from various photographers, including Alfred Wertheimer and Bill Ray.
Next pages: Elvis comes off the train.

Above: Fans are gathered in the terminal and show their appreciation. The one above the middle arm of the MP carries a scrap book and a picture of Elvis and also appears on the next three pages.

Above: Picture *Life magazine*, October 6, 1958 issue.

Tom Diskins, Elvis and Tom Parker making their way through the crowd.

Above: Elvis on his way to the first press conference of the morning at the Brooklyn Army Terminal. He is carrying a book in his left hand, a gift by a fellow GI. There was one poem that deeply touched Elvis, titled "Should You Go First" that he related to his mother who had recently passed away while he was in basic training.

Excerpt of the Press Conference about the book:

Who was the author of the book you were carrying when you got off the train?
I had just gotten the book, sir. I don't know.
Where did you get it, somebody gave it to you as a gift?
One of the boys gave it to me on the train. The title of the book was "Poems That Touch The Heart."
Did any of them touch your heart? Have you had the chance to read it?
Yes, ma'am, I read a couple of poems in it. I read one in particular called "Should You Go First," which is a beautiful poem.
Do you prefer poetry to short stories?
Yes, ma'am, I do.
Do you know by whom the poem was?
The author was unknown in the poem, that's right.

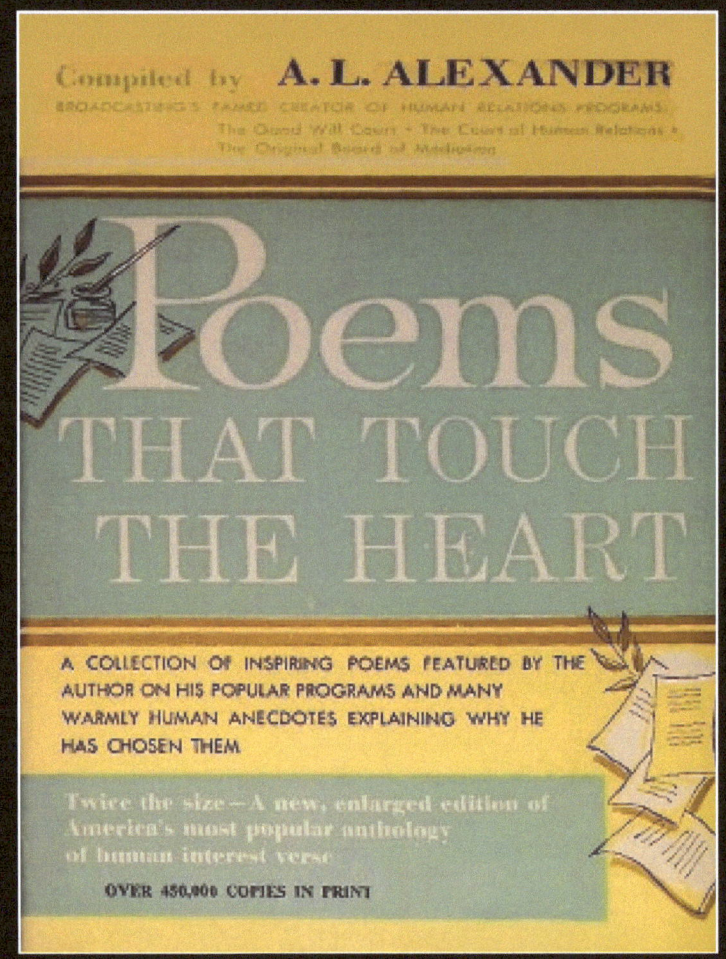

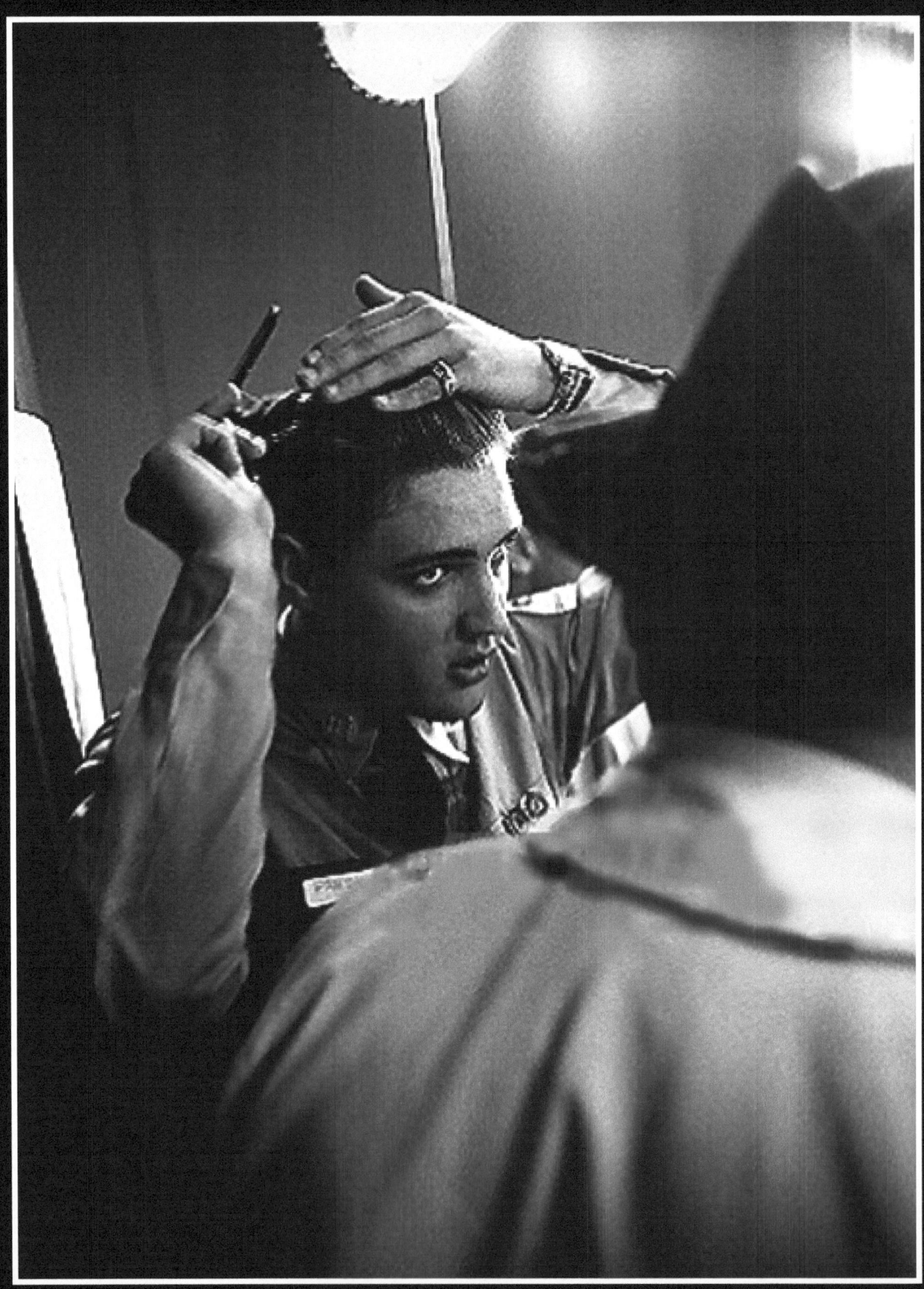

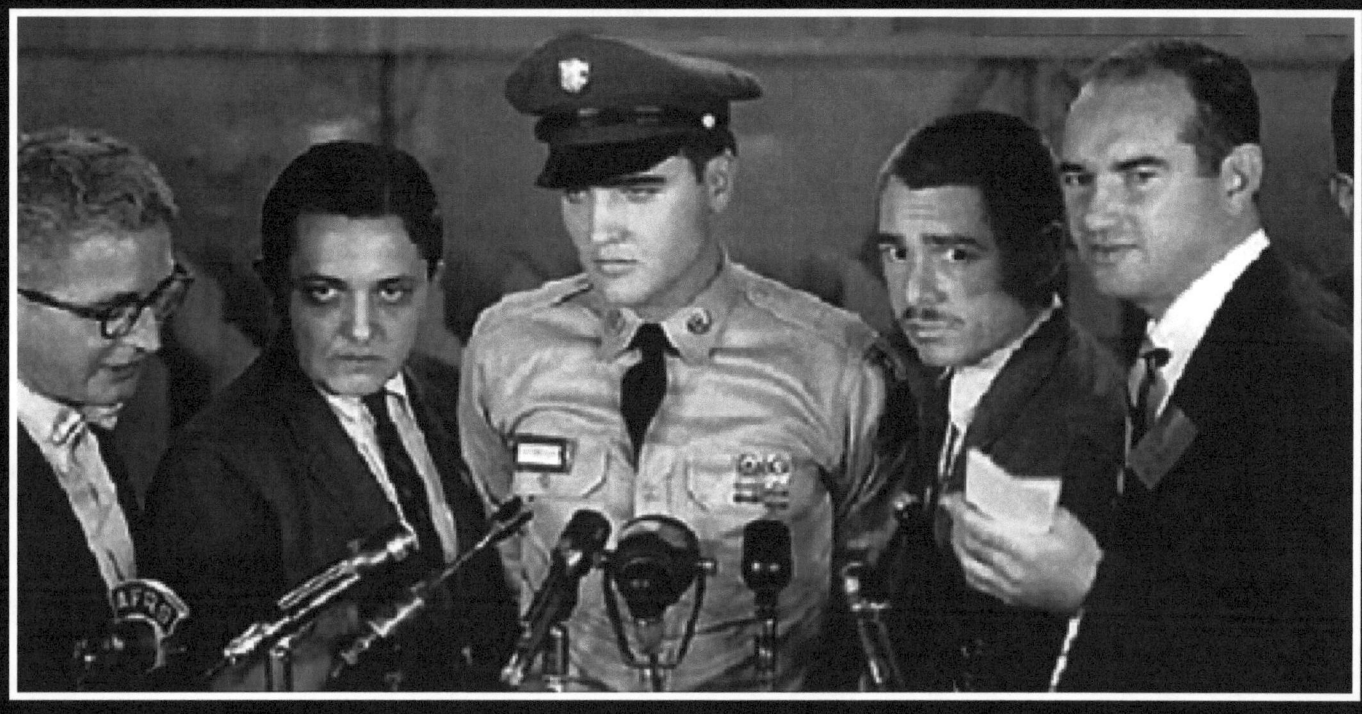

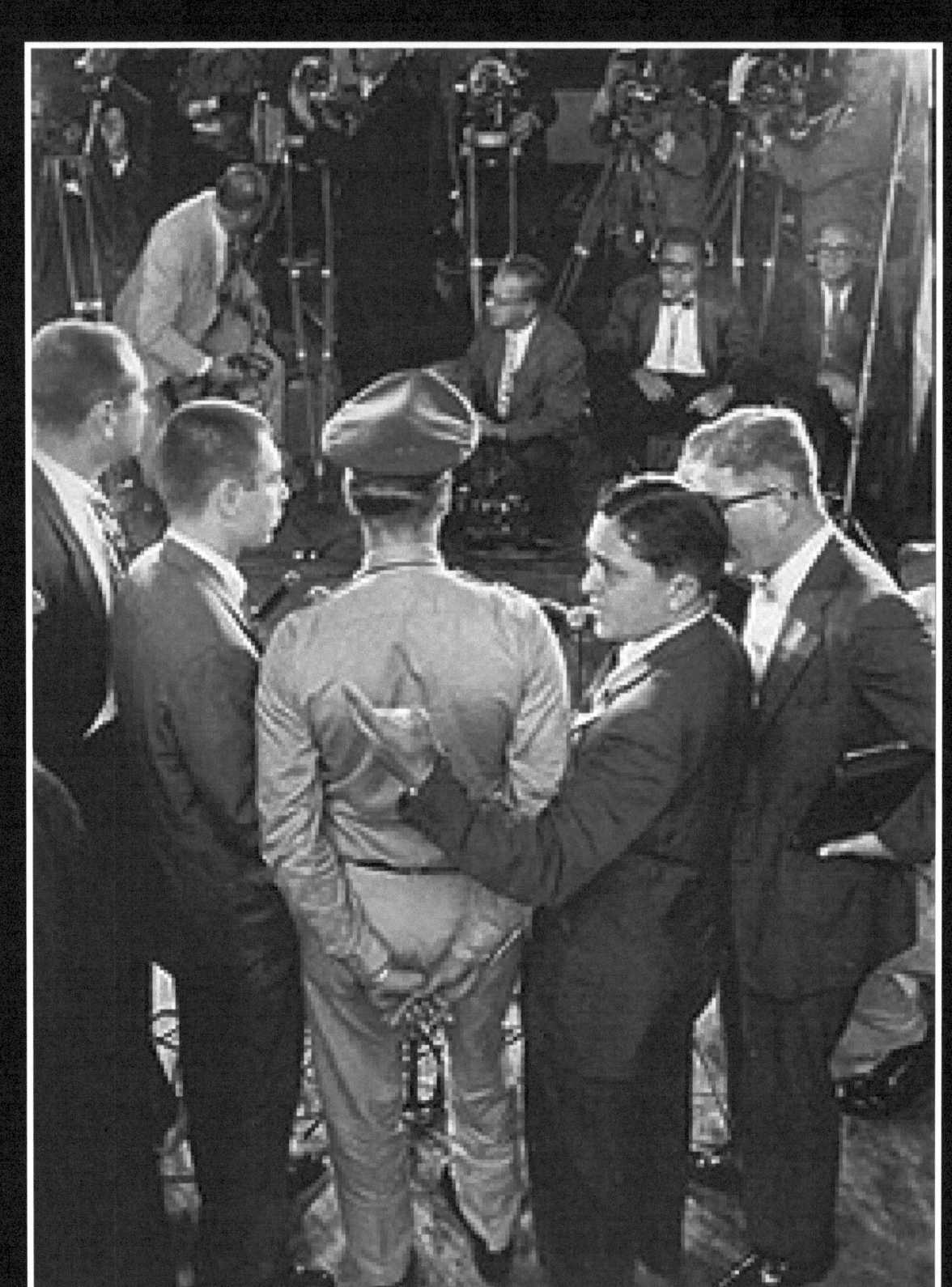

During the first conference, Elvis was surrounded by RCA Victor management, representatives from the William Morris Agency and of course Tom Parker and some members of his staff.

65

Getting ready for the main press conference.

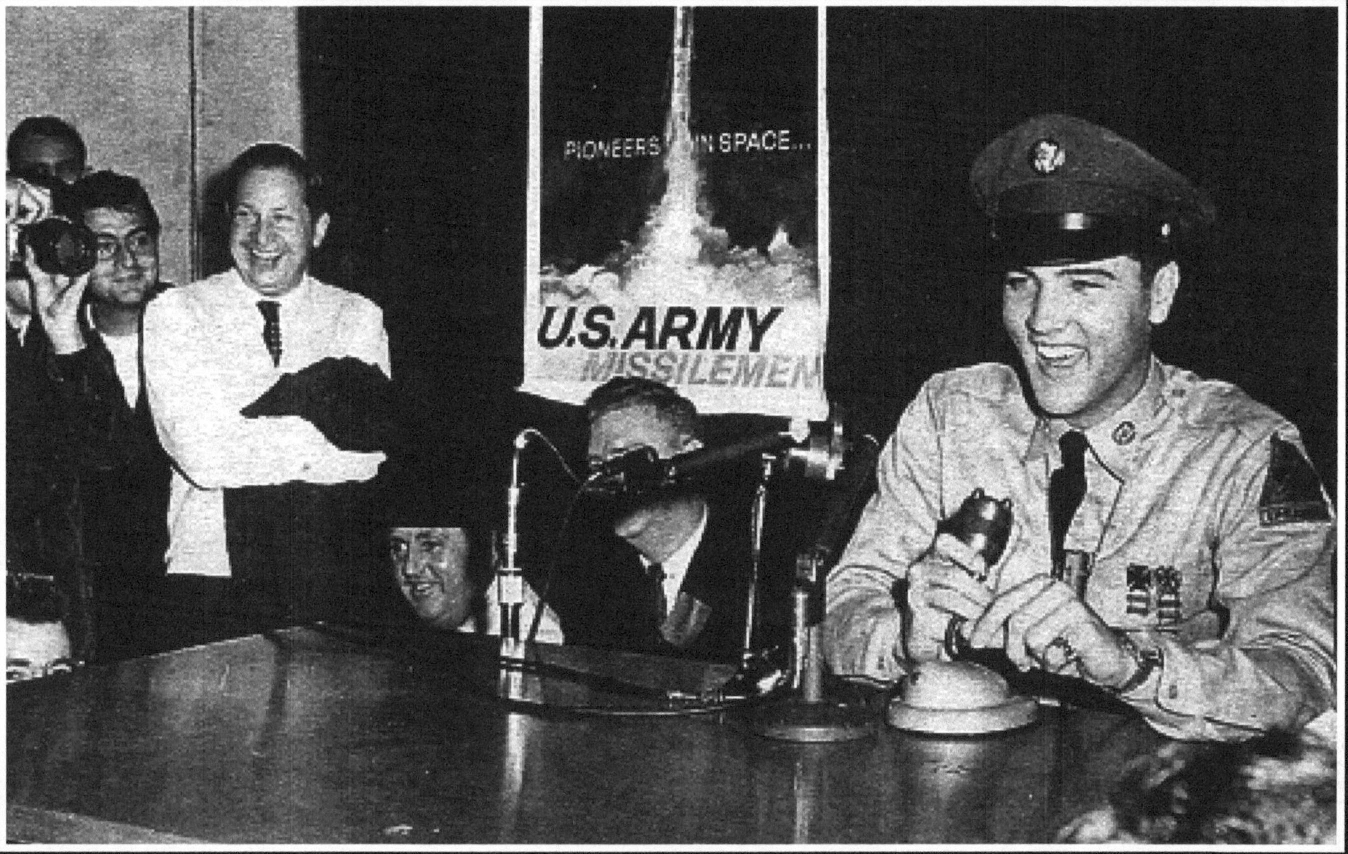
PIONEERS IN SPACE...
U.S. ARMY
MISSILEMEN

U.S.ARMY
AFRS

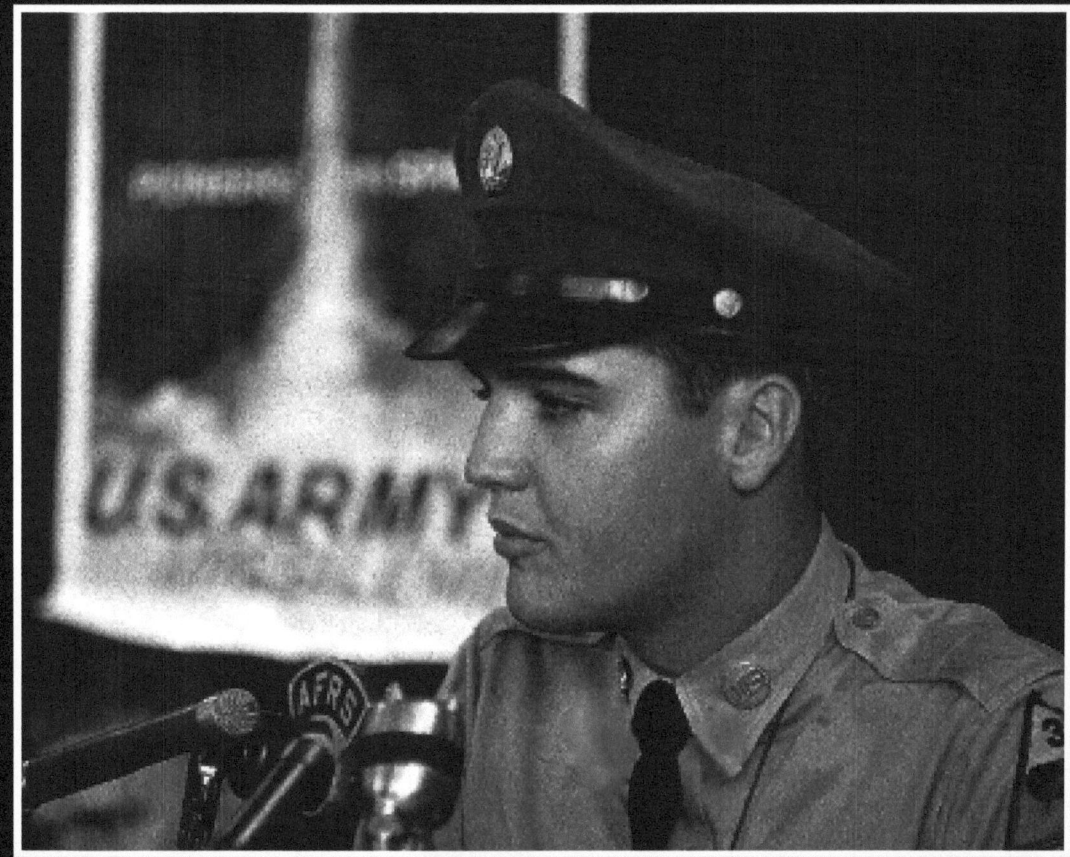

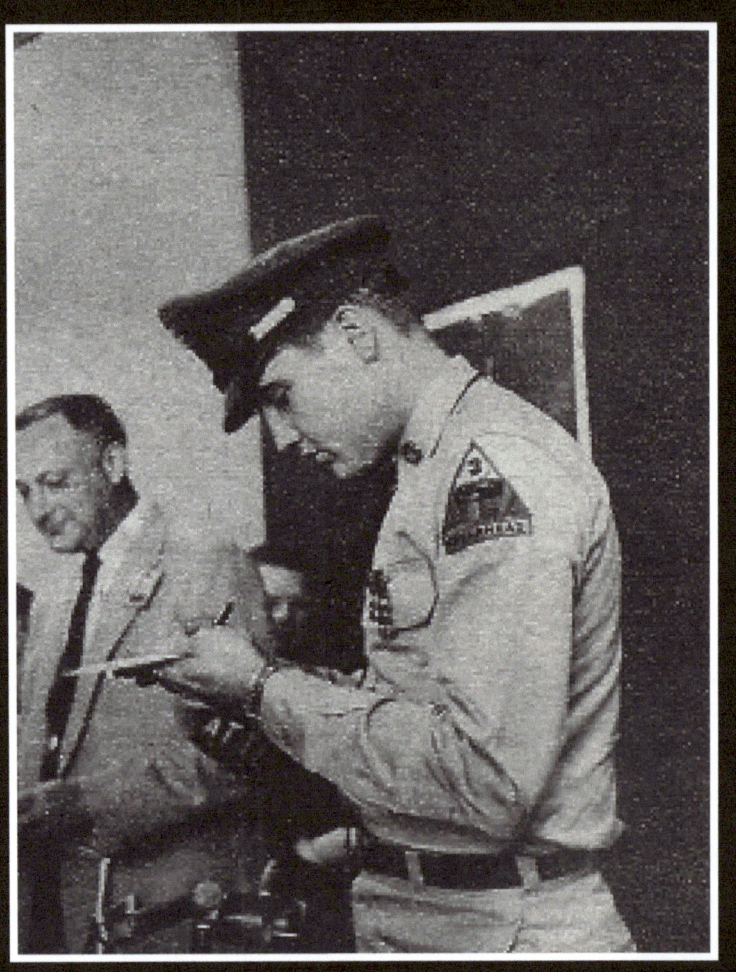

Here at the Brooklyn P.O.E. where Elvis Presley, Private Elvis Presley of the United States Army, is due to embark for Germany today. And let me tell you a little of what the hub-hub is like here. We've been, as I say, waiting for the past two hours for Presley to come in. There was some delay with his train… and he has just stepped off the elevator, which has brought him up from the lower level where many of his fellow embarkees have been preparing to go aboard the General Randall, the ship that he will take out to Germany.

Now Elvis moves over and is going to sit down behind the desk. The microphones will be brought in. More pictures will be taken. Elvis apparently enjoying the whole thing very much, he's been smiling since he walked into the room.

Ma'am.

What are your medals for?
It is all right to stand up, sir? These medals right here, ma'am, are for expert with a carbine rifle and also tank weapons.

What?
Tank weapon. That's a ninety-millimeter gun. And this one right here, I didn't do quite as well. It's the pistol. I got a sharpshooter over there (pointing to another soldier).

A forty-five?
Yes, sir, that's right.

Elvis, what do you think about going to Germany?
Well, sir, I'm kind lookin' forward to it.

Do you speak any German at all?
No, ma'am, I don't.

Are you planning to learn a little bit?
I'll probably have to in order to survive in Germany.

What does the "A" in your name stand for?
Aron.

Who was the author of the book you were carrying when you got off the train?
I had just gotten the book, sir. I don't know.

Where'd you get it? Somebody gave it to you as a gift?
One of the boys gave it to me on the train. The title of the book was A.L. Alexander's Poems That Touch the Heart.

Did any of them touch your heart? Have you had a chance to read it?
Yes, ma'am, I read a couple of poems in it. I read one in particular called "Should You Go First", which is a beautiful poem.

Do you prefer poetry to short stories?
Yes, ma'am, I do.

Do you know by whom the poem was?
The author was unknown in the poem. That's right.

Elvis, is your dad going to Germany shortly after or at the same time you do?
Yes, ma'am, he is supposed to leave, I think, on the twenty-sixth.

Elvis, most people have a song that is sort of special to them. Do you have a favourite song?
My favourite song is a song called "Padre." Are you familiar with it, by Tony Arden? And also, "You'll Never Walk Alone" was always one of my very favorites.

Elvis, do you think your high school R.O.T.C. did you any good in the Army?
Yes, ma'am, it definitely did. I knew my left leg from my right one and it helped quite a bit.

Did that color guard that you outfitted at Humes High School in Memphis give you any going away presents?
Yes, ma'am, they gave me an old musket – one of the old rifles, you know, you had to pack the powder in the end of it.

From the Civil War or before that?
I think it was the Civil War.

Your family's been here a long time. Were any of your ancestors in the Civil War, or the Revolution War?
Ah, let me see. On which side, let's see?

Do you still have your four Cadillacs?
Three now, sir. I traded one for a Lincoln, sir.

Are you going to take any of your cars with you?
No, ma'am. I'll get a German… when in Germany, do as the Germans do. I'll probably get a German car.

Don't you have one… a Messerschmitt?

I had one. I gave it away, sir.

How is it possible that you're not in the Special Services?
Ma'am, I don't know.

It's not your choice? I mean, no one asked you?
I haven't said anything. I mean, I guess the Army knows what's best for me.

What kind of work do they have you doing? What kind of work do you do generally?
Well, for about eighteen weeks I was in the tanks. I was a tank commander. And then the last few weeks I was there I was a truck driver. I drove a truck.

Elvis, should rock and roll die out between now and the time you get out of the service…
I'll starve to death, sir. I beg your pardon, sir.

What do you think you might do?
If rock and roll music were to die out – which I don't think it will – I would try something else. I would probably try… I would really probably go in for the movies then and I would try to make it as an actor, which is very tough 'cause you got a lot of competition.

Elvis, are you surprised that you're as big a success and as lasting a success as you are now? Did you think it was gonna turn out this well?
I didn't know, sir. I was hoping, but uh, I just took every day as it came along. I didn't anticipate that I was gonna, I was gonna do well, or I didn't anticipate I was gonna die

out.

How many Gold Records do you have, incidently?
Twenty-five, sir.

Twenty-five? That's tops, isn't it, in the business? Paramount says eight.
Eight? Sir, they're behind time.

Twenty-five?
I have twenty-five-million-sellers and two albums that have sold a million each. In fact, the RCA Victor men are here. They can verify that. Isn't that right?
(Colonel Tom Parker). Mr. Sholes is right here.
They've all disappeared, sir. Isn't that right, Mr. Sholes?
(Colonel Tom Parker) The gentleman with the red badge over there.

Do you plan to make any records while you're on furlough in Germany? I understand that's a privilege of all Army personnel.
I beg your pardon, sir.

Do you plan to make any records while you're on furlough in Germany? I understand that's a privilege of all Army personnel.
No, sir, I don't. I don't think so.

On the rock and roll, Elvis, do you think there's a sort of developing form of music? In other words, will it stay like it is or do you think it may change its form? Well, there's been criticism of the wiggling there. Do you think it's gonna straighten out or something like that? Do you know what I mean?
Sir, the wiggle can't straighten out. If you do, you're finished. It's like a guy down in Fort Hood… one of the sergeants one day… I was… I was sitting down on my foot locker and my left leg was shaking. I mean just unconsciously. He said, "Presley, I wish you'd quit shaking that leg". I said, "Sarge, when that leg quits shaking I'm finished."

You've probably seen that your fans brought down the ceiling in London when King Creole was showing last week. Do you plan to go to England at all on furlough from Germany?
I would like to, if I can make it on a three-day pass.

Elvis, what would you like to do the most on your first leave in Europe?
I'd like to go to Paris… and look up Brigitte Bardot.

Elvis, do you have anything you want to say to your many admirers before going overseas… any farewell word?
Yes, sir, I would. I'd like to say that I'm gonna do my best to keep putting out the records and everything they enjoy, and that I'll be looking forward to coming back and entertaining them again.

Do you have any records cut that are not released?
Yes, ma'am, I do.

How many?
I have two… or is it three. I don't know. He (Colonel Tom Parker) says it's four.

Could you tell me what you think of Dean Martin's "Volare", and the Italian singers that have come along?
I think it's great. I went out and bought the

Do you think you might record something like that?
Me record an Italian song? I don't know if I could cut the mustard.

While you're in the service, do you plan to take advantage of any of the educational benefits given by the armed services?
Well, I have heard a lot about the different types of schooling the Army has to offer. And I do know for a fact that a lot of fellows have gone through the service and benefited out in the civilian life, after they come out of the service. A lot of guys that had nothing prior to the time they went in, and they go in the service and they take some kind of schooling for maybe a year or two years and when they come out of the Army, well, they're qualified for a good job. Now, it doesn't hurt for anybody to have a profession to turn to in case something did happen to the entertainment business, or something happen to me. I don't know exactly yet what kind of a school that I would like to go to.

Elvis, on the trip here, on the trip here on the train from wherever you took off from…
Fort Hood, sir…

Fort Hood to here in Brooklyn, you must have some time to yourself. What did you think about?
Well, there were three hundred and fifty guys on the train with me. They didn't give me much time to think. You know, the boys come around and they talk. They wan to know about Hollywood and different things. They want to know about making movies and things. We pretty well kept occupied. I don't like to sit alone too much and think.

Have you formed any real close buddies in the service, friendships since you been in?
Yes, sir, I've got quite a few buddies in there.

Elvis, are you sorry you never got to college?
Right at the time, we didn't have enough money to go to college. I would have liked to have gone.

Would you like to go back at some point?
Well, it's according to what the future holds for me.

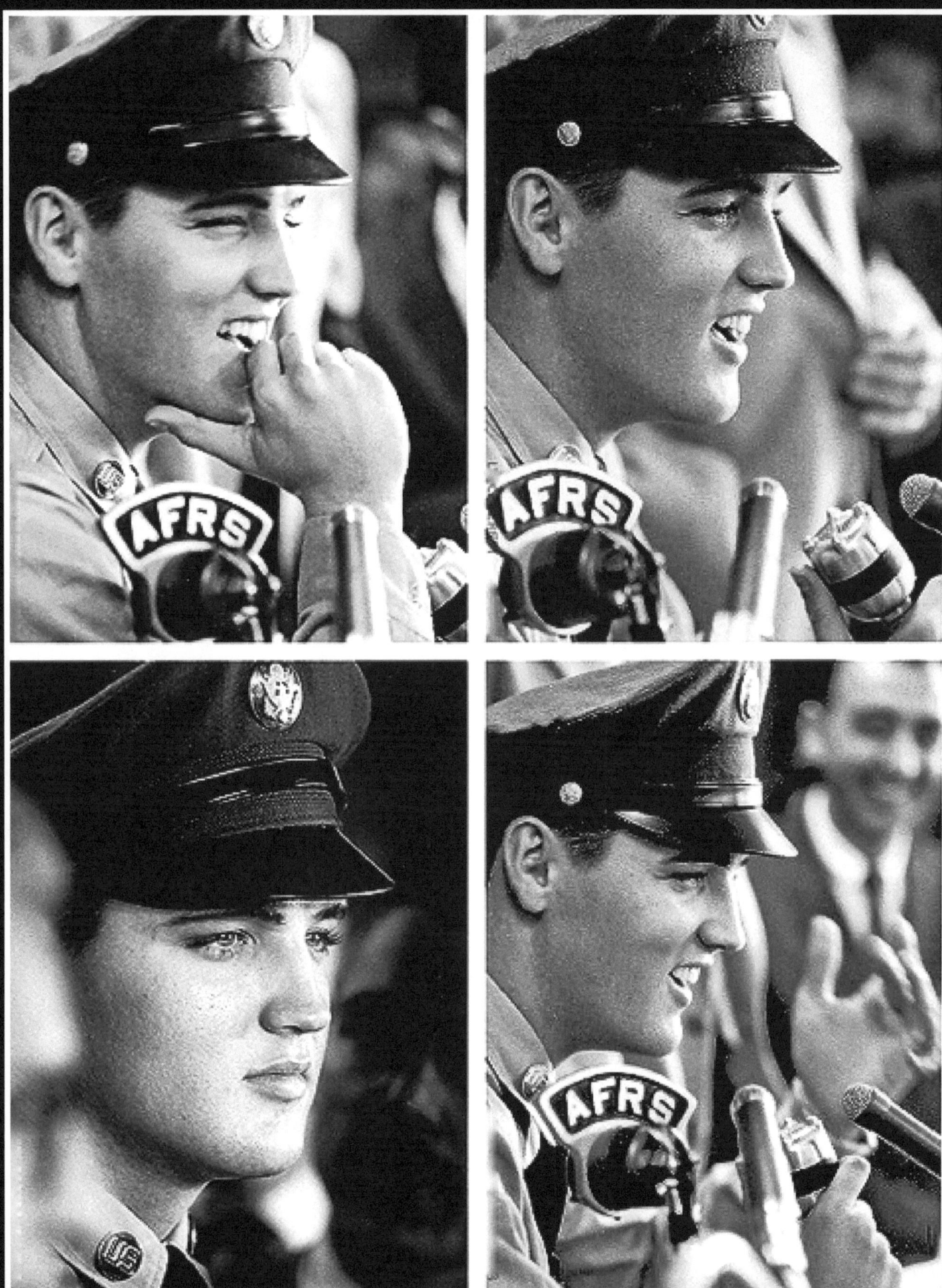

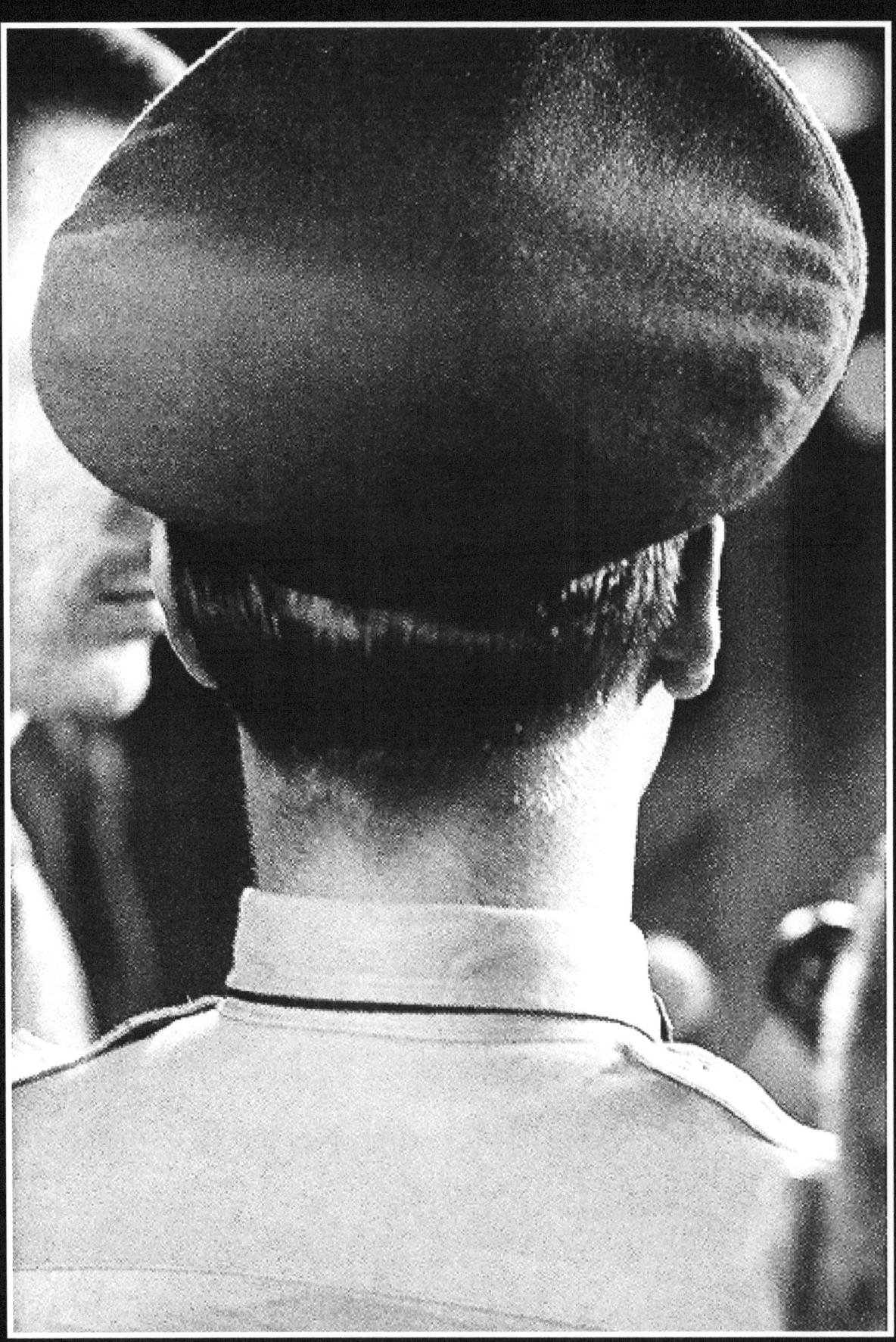

Elvis signing autographs for fellow soldiers.

Opposite: *The New York Times*, September 23, 1958.

94

PRIVATE PRESLEY SAILS

Singer Leaves for 18-Month Army Hitch in Germany

Pvt. Elvis Presley departed yesterday with 1,170 members of the Third Armored Division for an eighteen-month tour of duty in Germany. The entertainer said that if rock 'n' roll music died out during his stay in service, he would give up singing and try to become a good actor.

The popular singer arrived at the Brooklyn Army Base with troops from Fort Hood, Tex., and boarded the transport Randall for the trip to Bremerhaven. About 100 teen-age girls had gathered earlier outside the gates of the base to see Private Presley, but the troops got off the train too far away.

The New York Times

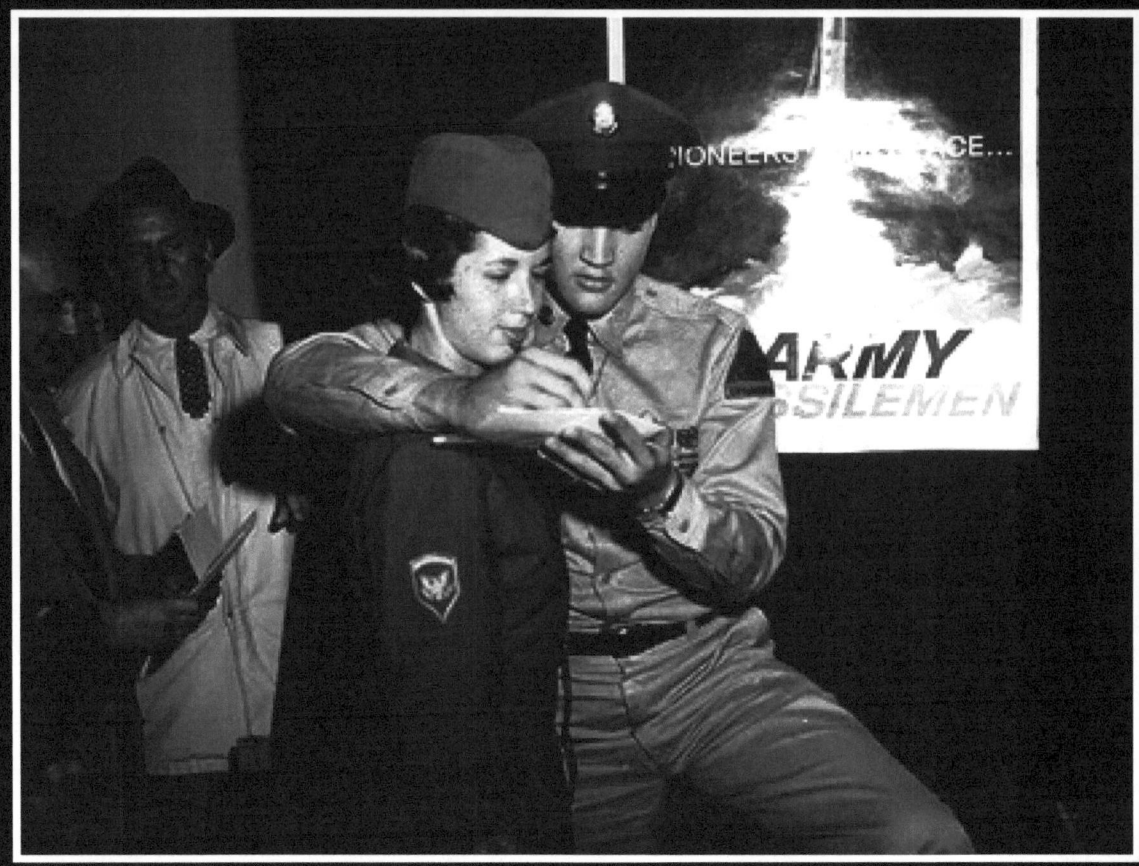

Elvis And Mary Davies WAC specialist from Albany, New York,

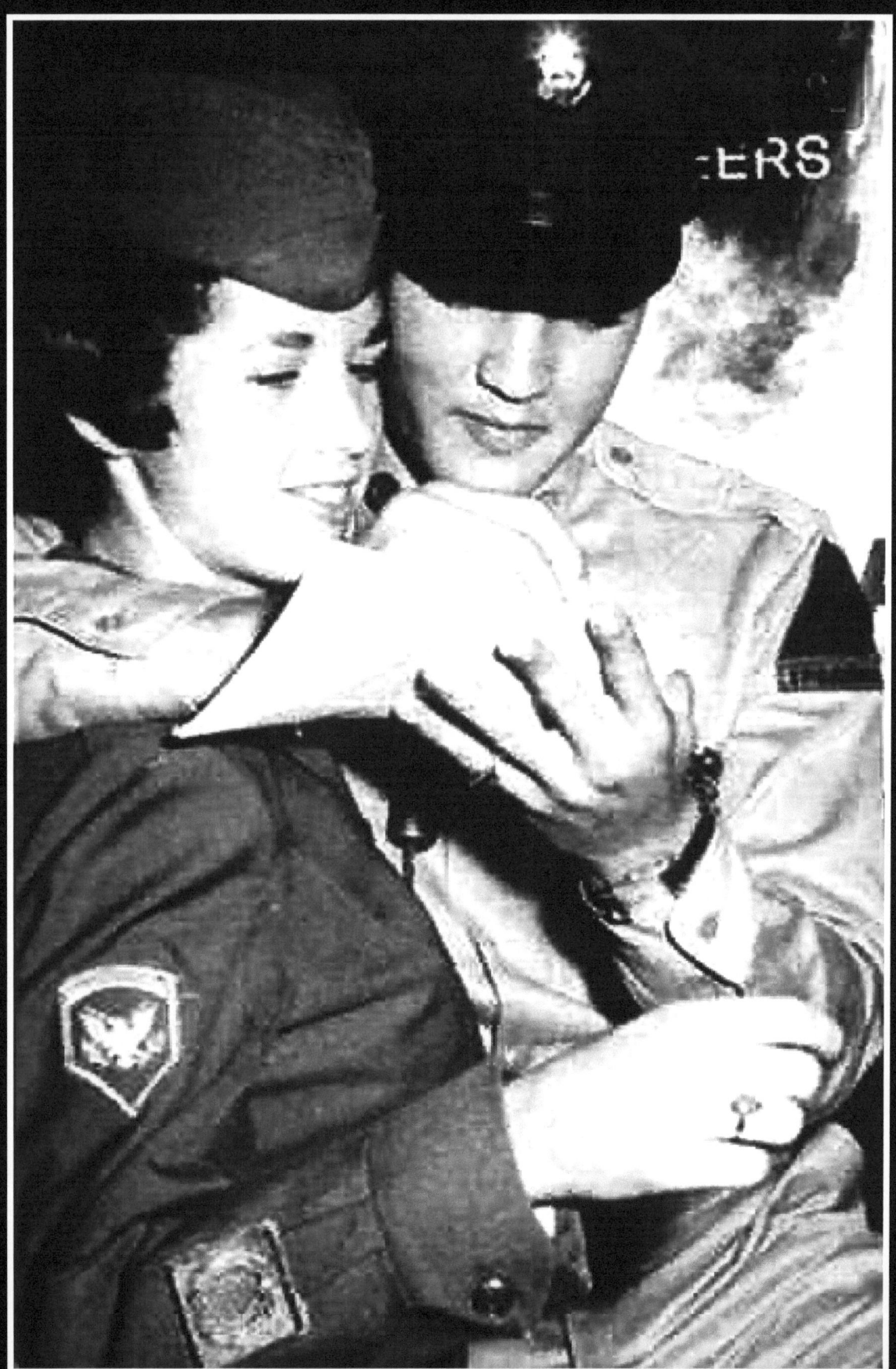

September 22, 1958

Elvis leaves from the Brooklyn Navy Yard for Germany.

This is what I remember of that day.

I was in the WAC's stationed at Fort Hamilton Army Base in Brooklyn, New York. A Public Relations lady stopped by my desk and asked me if I'd like to go to a press conference for Elvis. I said "sure, let's go".

When we got there the room was absolutely packed with reporters and photographers. We were way in the back of the room but Elvis saw us and at one point, he pointed at me and motioned for me to come up front.

Then it was like the Red Sea parting. All the press, etc. moved to one side or the other and a wide aisle opened up.

I walked up to Elvis, who was smiling and very charming. He told me to move to his other side...that was his "good" side. He put his arm around my shoulders and signed the press release. Then he signed it again as the photographers kept asking for more shots.

It was a very memorable moment for me. He seemed to be a very kind, gentle and warm person.

The next day those pictures were on the front pages of almost every American newspaper.

Mary Davies Germond

Mary Davies Germond

Mary Davies' recollection of this day. Source: http://www.elvis-collectors.com

101

The hoards of photographers and cameramen wanted to get film of Elvis going up the ramp from the dock to the second deck of the ship. Five soldiers were selected to join Elvis in the shot to make it look natural. Of course, Elvis was carrying going-away presents as well as his duffel bag. Courtesy Dr. John Carpenter, http://www.elvis-collectors.com

All in all, Elvis had to walk the gangways eight times, shouldering a borrowed duffel bag in order to satisfy the bevy of cameramen and photographers present to put this historical departure on film.

Elvis boards the ship for the second time, now with gifts and another soldier's bag as a prop.

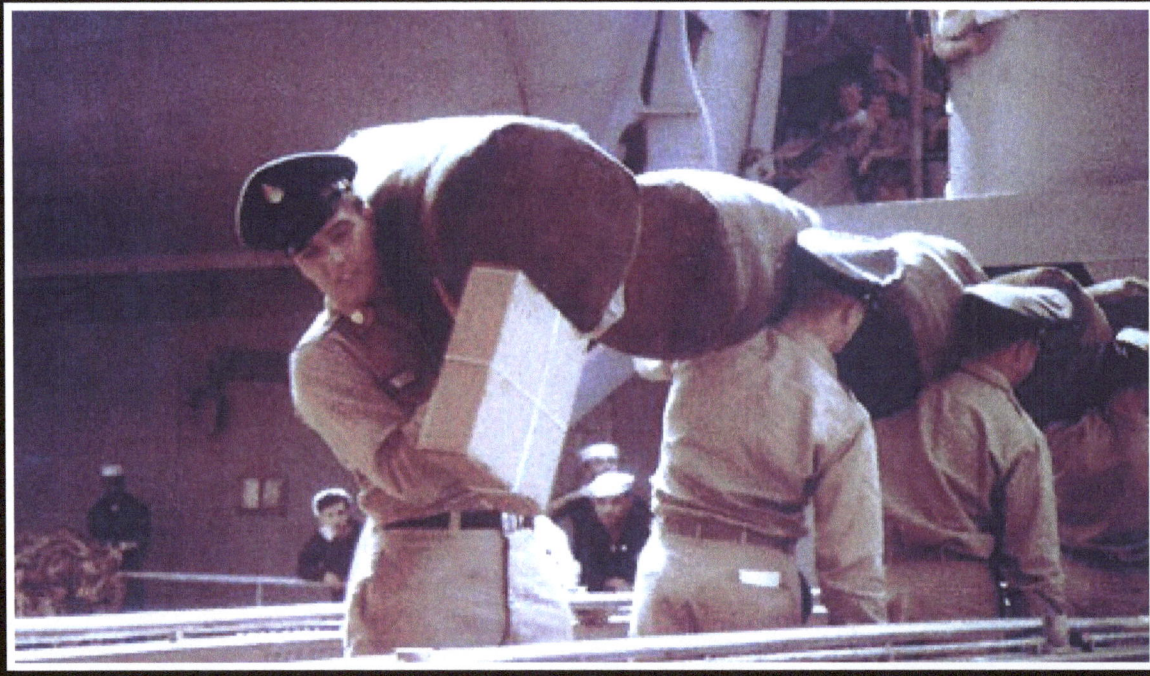

Elvis' first contact with Lillian Portnoy. Later she would get Elvis' second most famous kiss ever photographed.

Above: Elvis returns to gangway to look for Lillian Portnoy.
Opposite: Lillian Portnoy somehow followed Elvis to the gangway

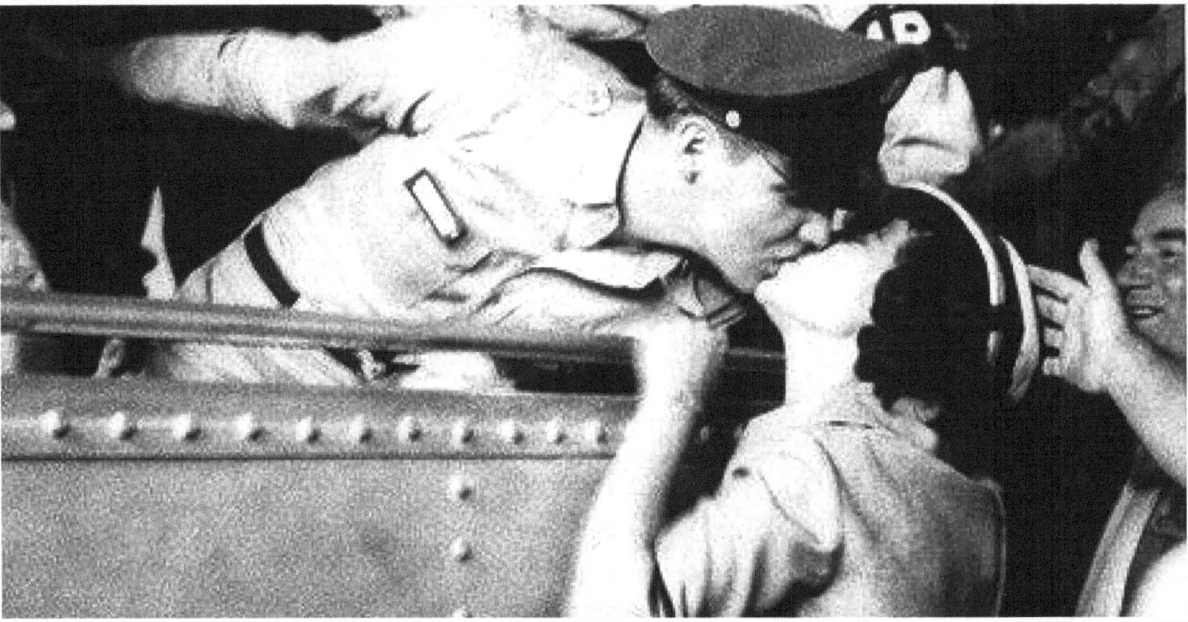

Elvis kissing fan Lillian Portnoy. Some photographs by Bill Ray. This was the second kiss. Elvis lost his cap during the first one and was asked to reenact the scene. He pleasantly obliged. Then it was Lillian who lost her hat. Last picture opposite.

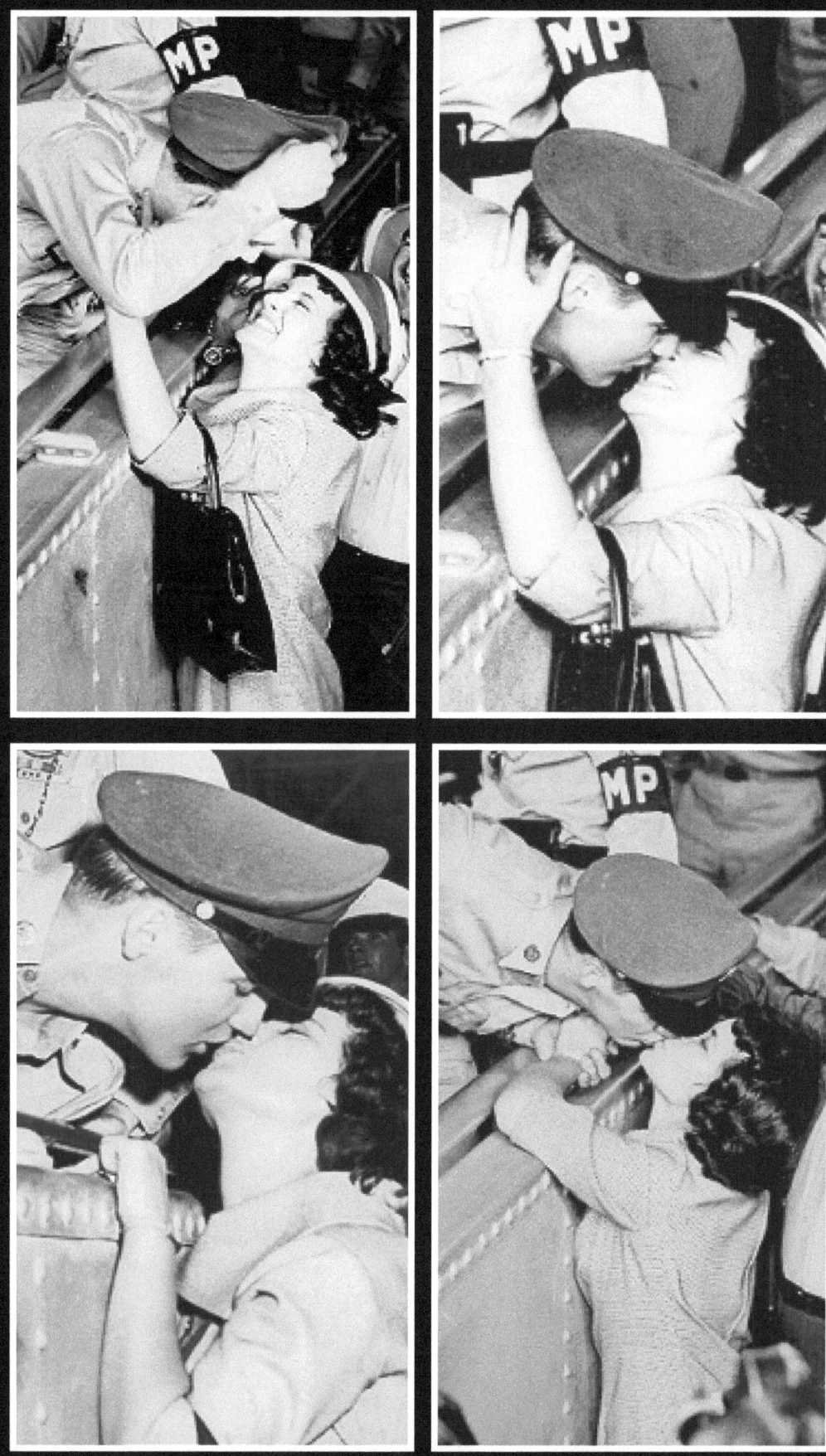

115

Welcome aboard.

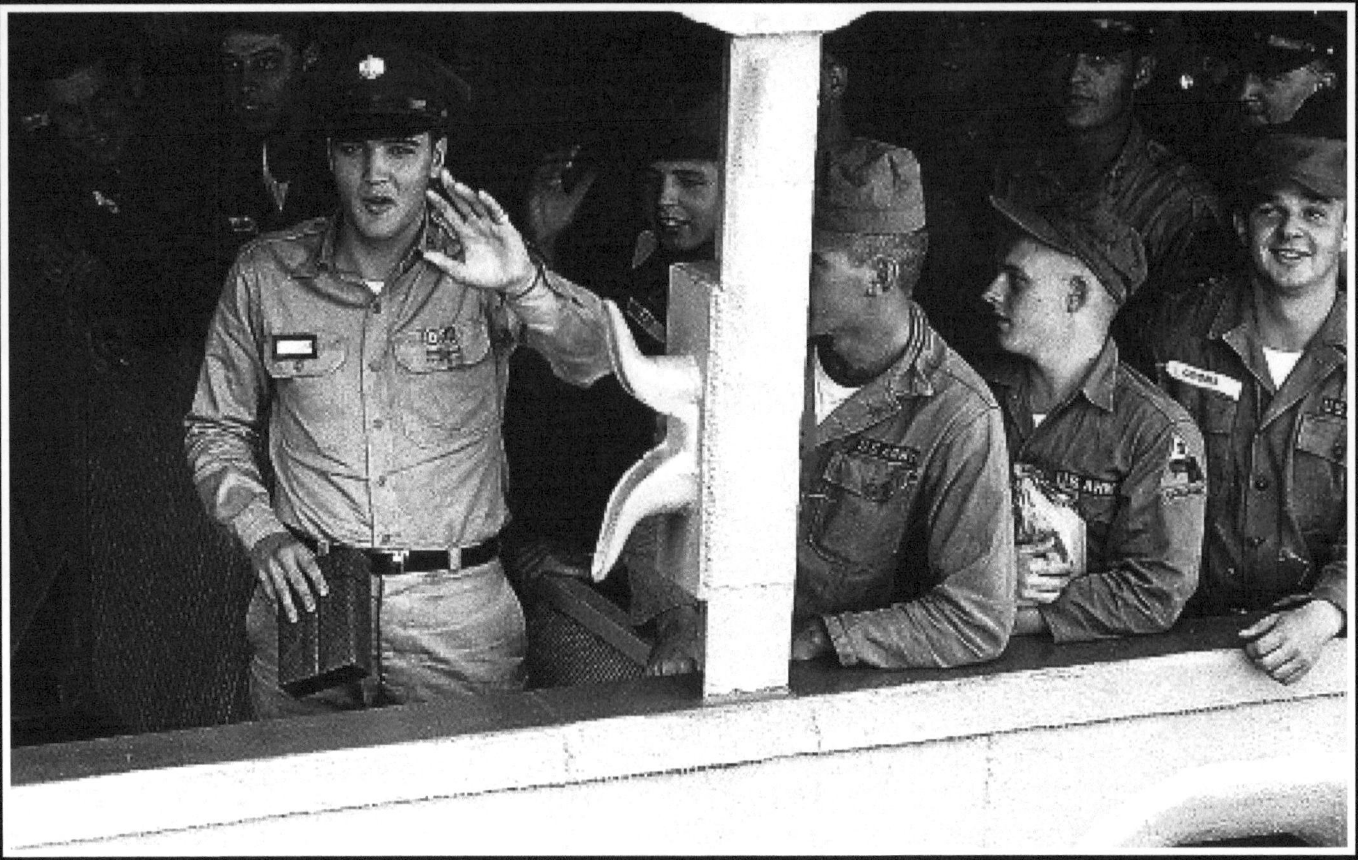
U.S. ARMY

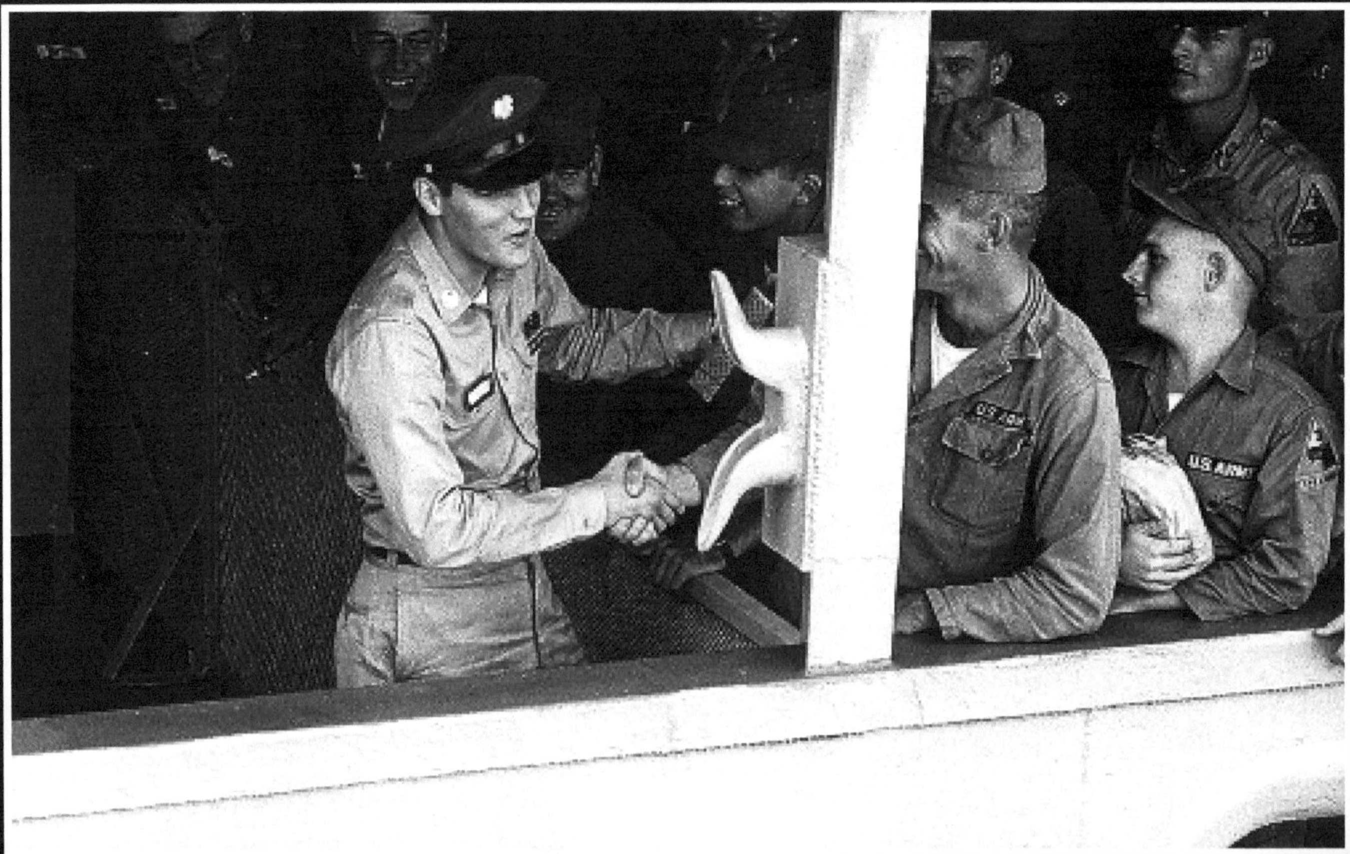
U.S. ARMY

127

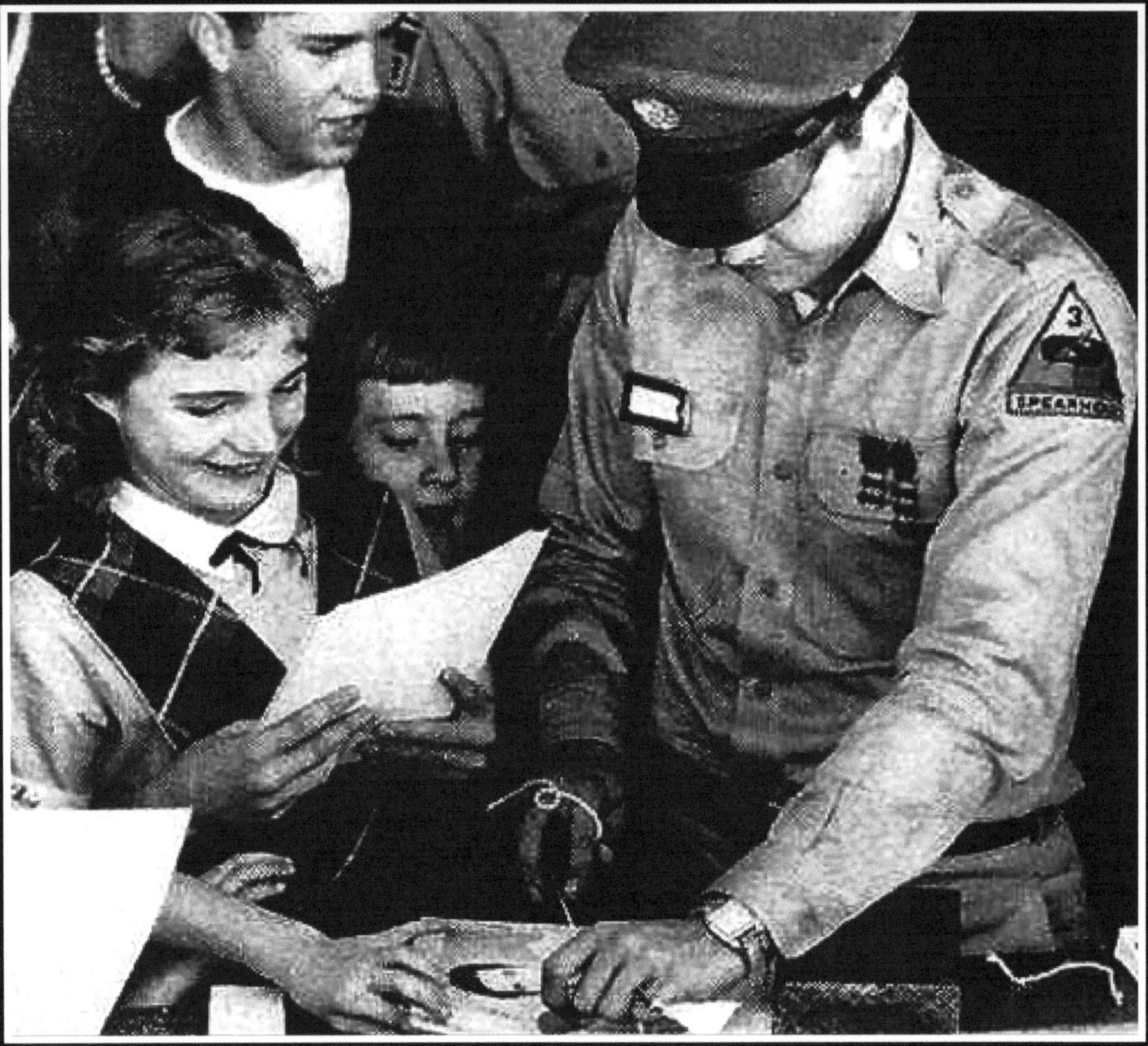

The Brooklyn Army Terminal was most heavily trafficked during World War II, during which more than 20,000 military and civilian personnel were employed there. The Terminal was the headquarters and nerve center for the New York Port of Embarkation, a region-wide operation covering more than a dozen facilities that moved 3.2 million troops and 37 million tons of military supplies to fronts across the globe. Arguably the most famous soldier to deploy from The Brooklyn Army Terminal was Elvis Presley, when he shipped off from Brooklyn to Germany.

135

Alfred Wertheimer recalled: The ship had four decks and soon Elvis appeared on the top one – along with Col. Parker. Wertheimer wondered to himself, "What is Parker doing on a troop ship?" To give something to Elvis, it turned out. Elvis opened a box from Parker, and guess what it contained? Dozens of playing-card-sized autographed photos of Elvis. Then, Elvis tossed them one-by-one over the railing, and they fluttered down to lucky fans standing on the dock four decks below as the band played "Hound Dog." Just your average troop deployment.

Courtesy Dr. John Carpenter, http://www.elvis-collectors.com

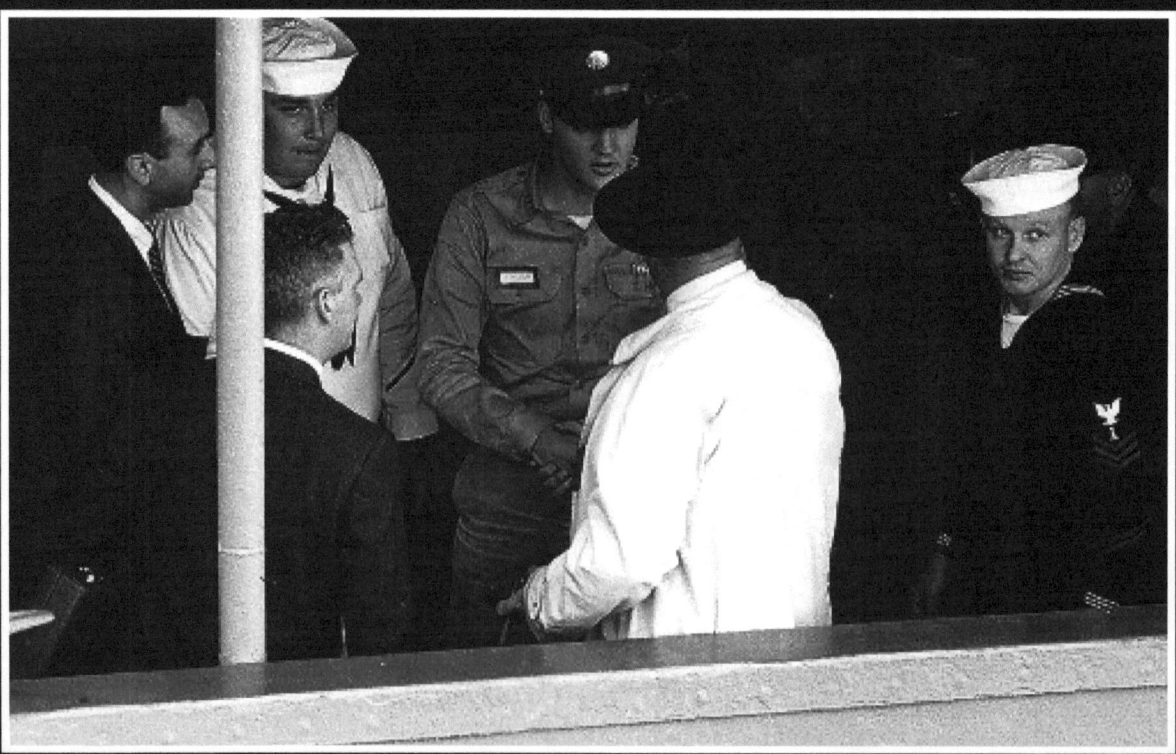

Opposite bottom: Elvis saying goodbye to Tom Parker, presumably.

PRIVATE PRESLEY SAILS

Singer Leaves for 18-Month Army Hitch in Germany

Pvt. Elvis Presley departed yesterday with 1,170 members of the Third Armored Division for an eighteen-month tour of duty in Germany. The entertainer said that if rock 'n' roll music died out during his stay in service, he would give up singing and try to become a good actor.

The popular singer arrived at the Brooklyn Army Base with troops from Fort Hood, Tex., and boarded the transport Randall for the trip to Bremerhaven. About 100 teen-age girls had gathered earlier outside the gates of the base to see Private Presley, but the troops got off the train too far away.

The New York Times
Copyright © The New York Times
Originally published September 23, 1958

Elvis had an interview with journalist Pat Hernon in the library of the ship just moments before it sailed away to Germany.

The USS Randall leaving New York harbor waters. It departed the Brooklyn Army Terminal at 2:00 PM. It would reach Bremerhaven after 9 days at sea, arriving in the morning of October 1.

The extended play *Christmas With Elvis* was shipped by RCA on September 22. It was the second EP culled from the Chrismas album released the previous year. It sold 80,000 cop-

EPA-4340

SIDE 1
WHITE CHRISTMAS (Irving Berlin Music Corp., ASCAP 2:23)
HERE COMES SANTA CLAUS (Western Music Pub. Co., ASCAP 2:02)

SIDE 2
OH LITTLE TOWN OF BETHLEHEM P.D. 2:34
SILENT NIGHT P.D. 2:23

CHRISTMAS WITH ELVIS
ELVIS PRESLEY

You will also enjoy these EPs by Elvis Presley:

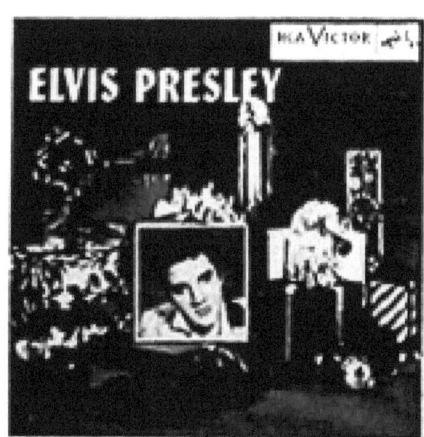

Elvis Sings Christmas Songs — EPA-4108

Peace in the Valley — EPA-4054

IMPORTANT NOTICE
This is a "New Orthophonic" High Fidelity recording, designed for the phonograph of today or tomorrow. Played on your present machine, it gives you the finest quality of reproduction. Played on a "Stereophonic" machine, it gives even more brilliant true-to-life fidelity. You can buy today, without fear of obsolescence in the future.

Elvis having a meal at the ship captain's table.

In the ship's library.

On the ship, Elvis and Charlie Hodge became good friends. At Elvis' request, they bunked together. They put on a show. Charlie acted as the Master of Ceremonies and Elvis played the piano, backing up the band. He did not sing.

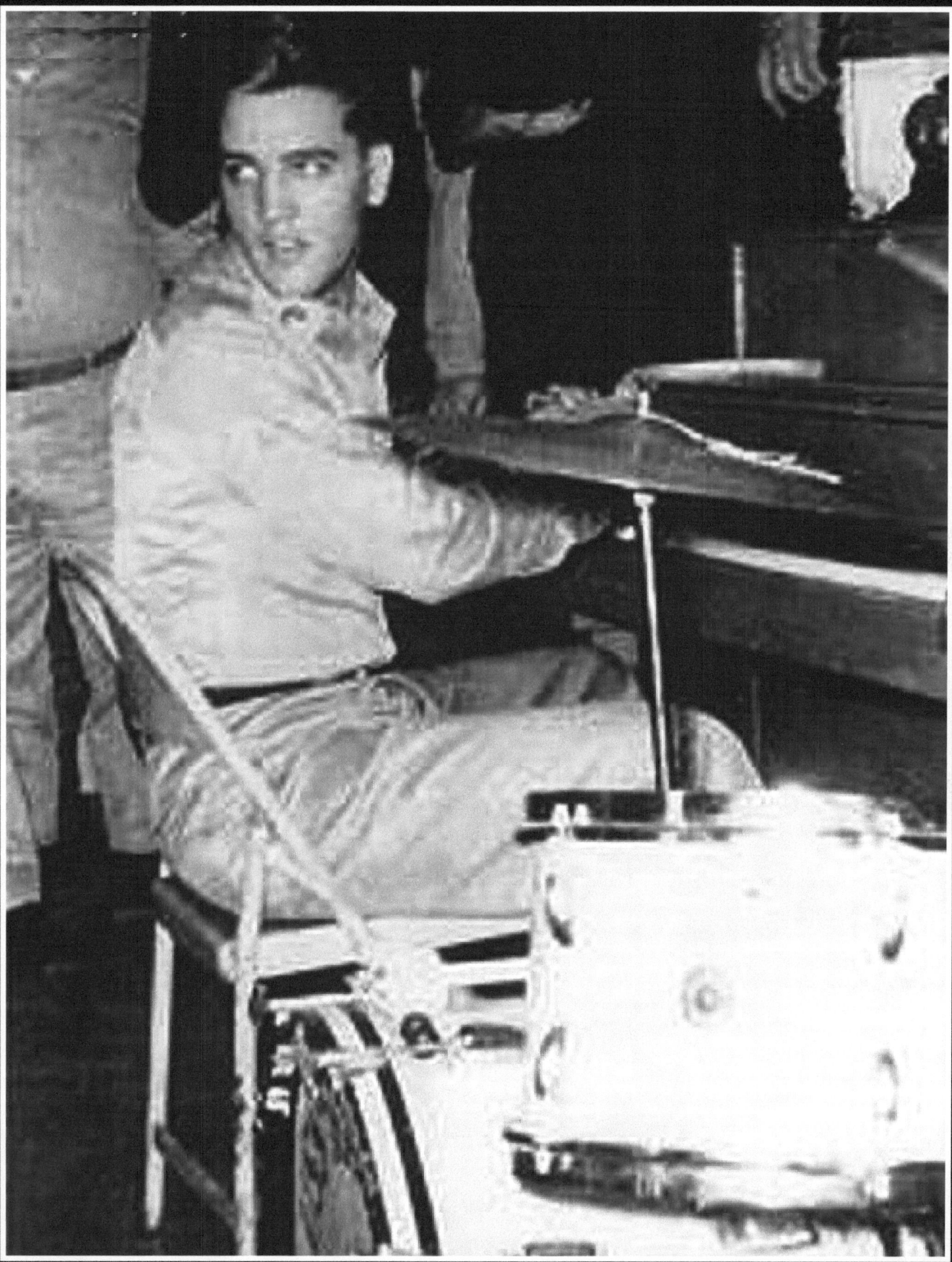

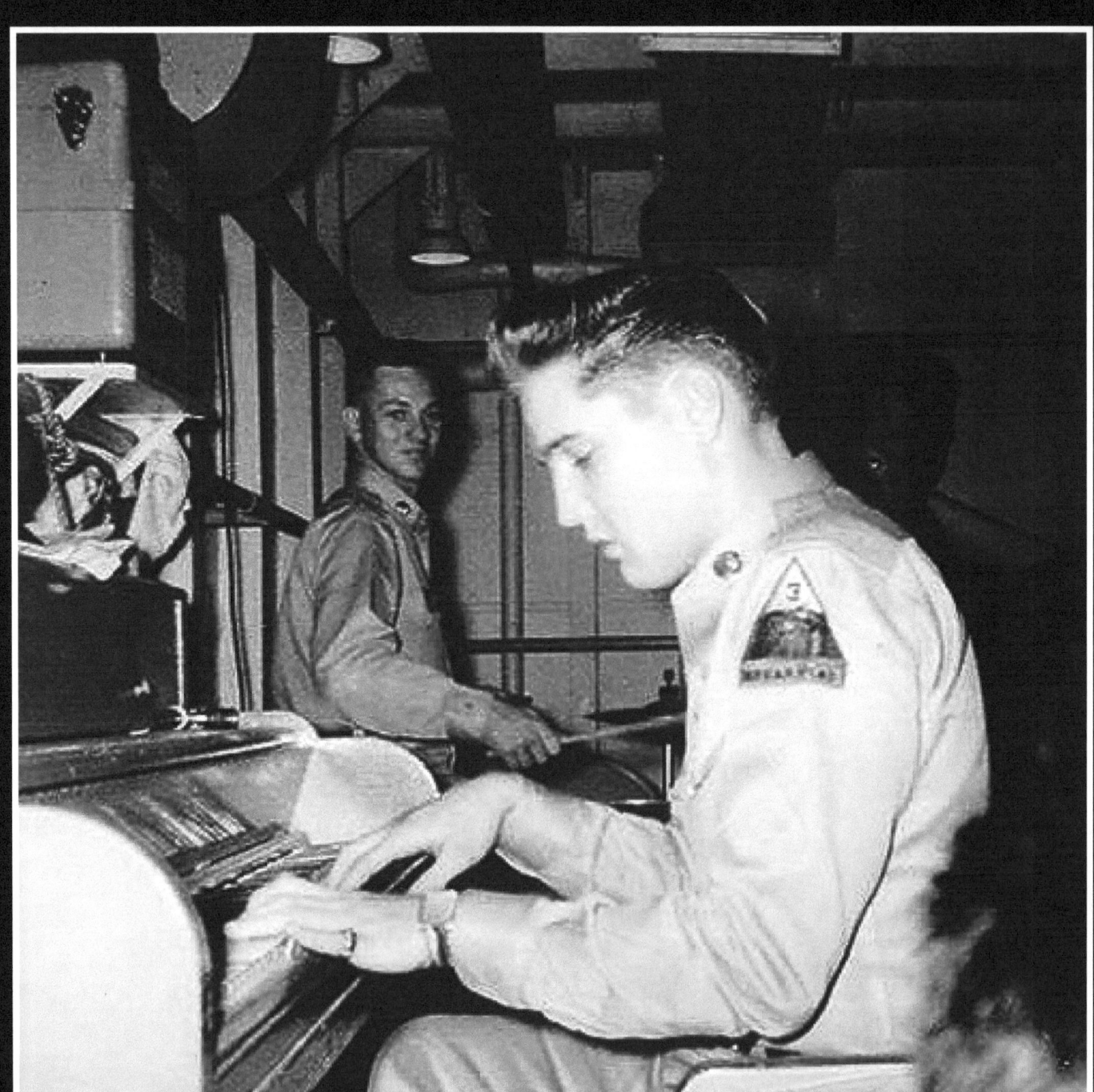

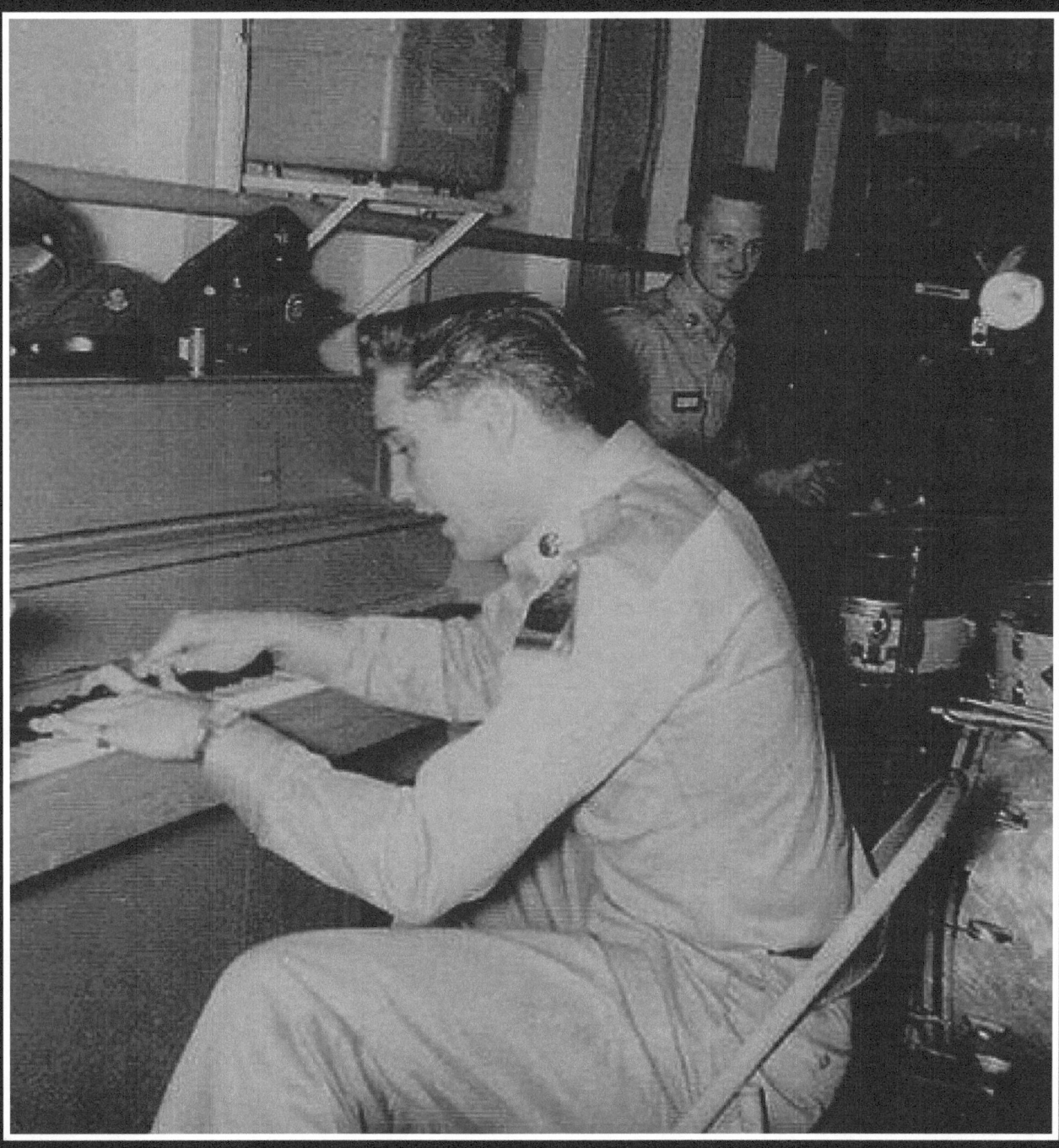

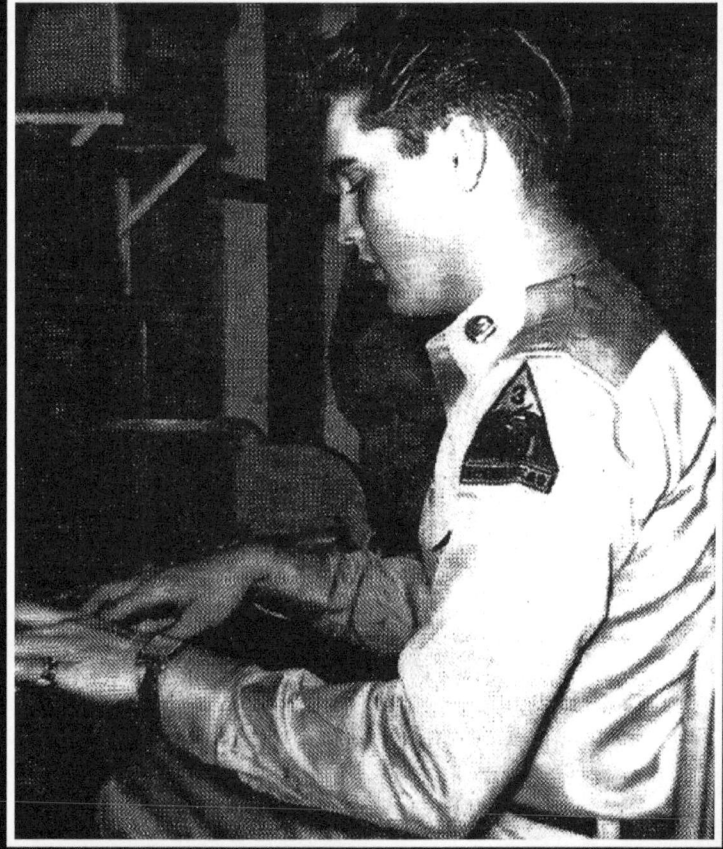

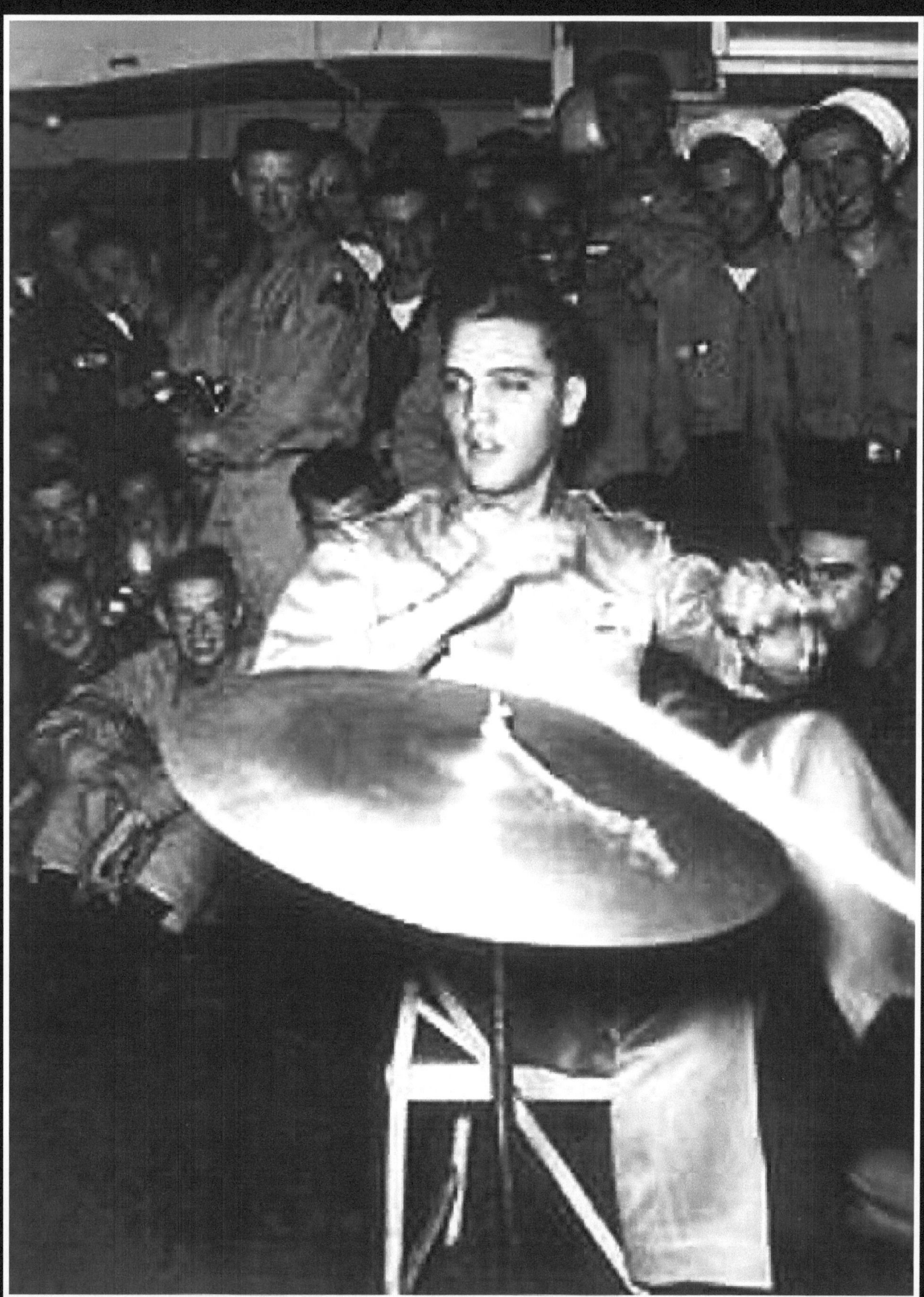

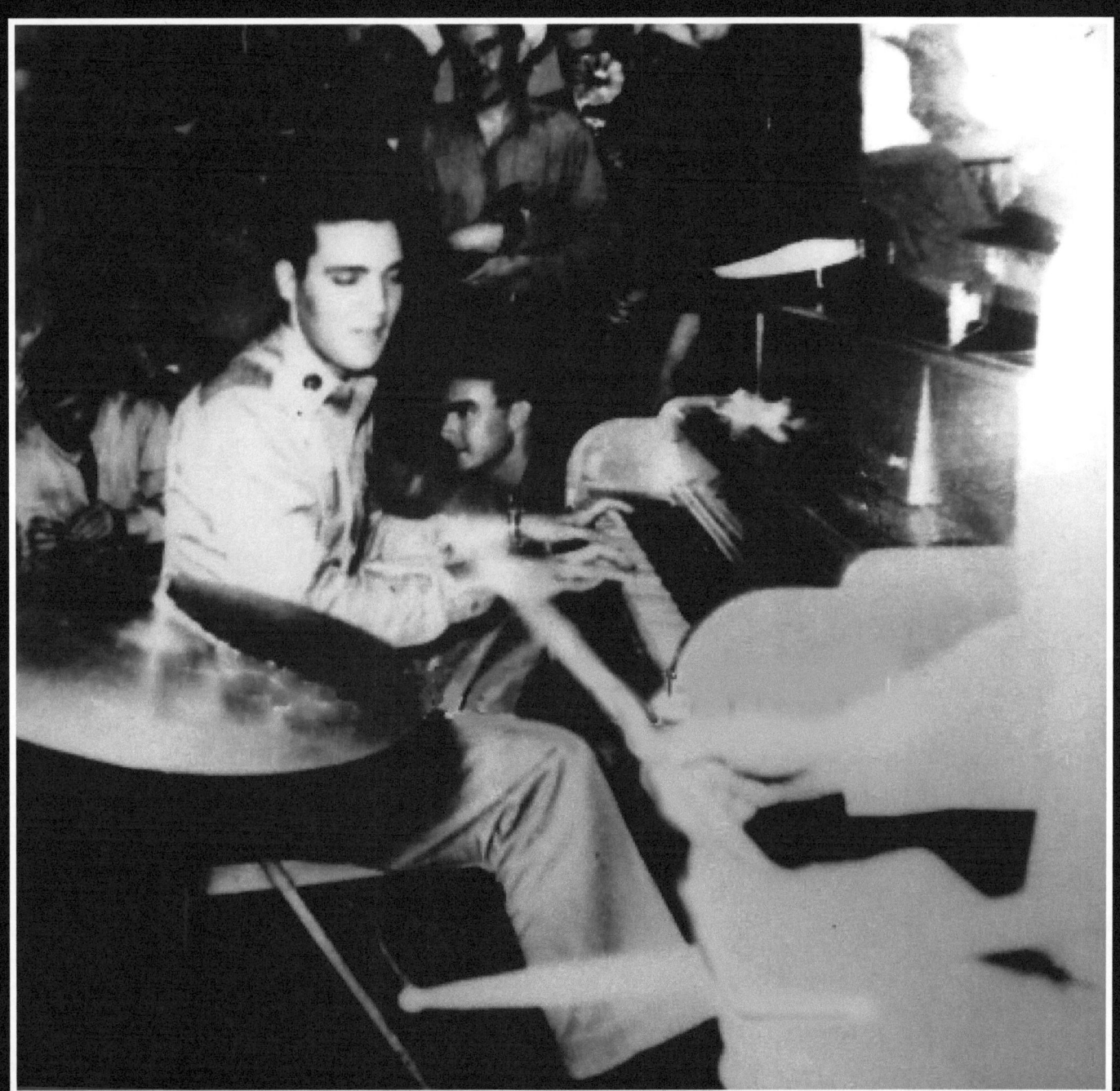

15/OCT/58

Hi SherryLee
 I received your letter and was very glad to hear that you are glad that I got you Elvis autograph.
 Well this is the way the story goes I went to breakfast. When I was done I wanted to go outside of the ship. So I was walking down the hall and I saw him coming the other way with a suitcase. And he was looking at my name tag and he couldn't make it out. So when I got near to him I said Hi and he asked me how to say it. And I told him. I asked him how he likes the Army and he said not for a darn. Then I said I got a "little" girl that would like to write to him. But then I told him that you are 17 yrs old. And I

show him the picture of you. He said that if he wrote to everybody that's all he would be able to do. So I asked him for his autograph and I had that card so I gave it to him and he sign it. Well that is all about Elvis. HO! You asked if he sang on the ship well he did not, but he did play the piano and boy he would play.
Well that is all for now And May God Bless You

Your Friend
Private

P.S. I guess I will not see Elvis again because he lives pretty far from me. He is a jeep driver

Letter dated October 15, 1958 from a soldier on the USS Randall to his friend.

Hi Sherry Lee,

I received your letter and was very glad to hear that you are glad that I got you an Elvis autograph.
Well this is the way the story goes. I went to breakfast. When I was done I wanted to go outside of the ship. So I was walking down the hall and I saw him coming the other way with a suitcase. And he was looking at my name tag and he couldn't make it out. So when I got near to him I said hi and he asked me how to say it. And I told him. I asked him how he liked the army and he said not for a darn. Then I said I got a "Little" girl that would like to write to him. But then I told him that you are 17 yrs old. And I show him the picture of you.
He said that if he wrote to everybody that's all he would be able to do. So I asked him for his autograph and I had that card so I gave it to him and he sign it. Well that is all about Elvis.
HO! You asked me if he sang on the ship well he did not but he did play the piano and boy he could play.
Well that is all for now. And-May-God-Bless-You.

Your friend

Private

P. S. I guess I will not see Elvis again because he lives pretty far from me. He is a jeep driver.

Source: Ebay

Interesting letter. The writer witnessed Elvis playing the piano during this show put on mostly by Charlie Hodge, adding that Elvis could really play! He also confirmed that Elvis did not sing during the show.

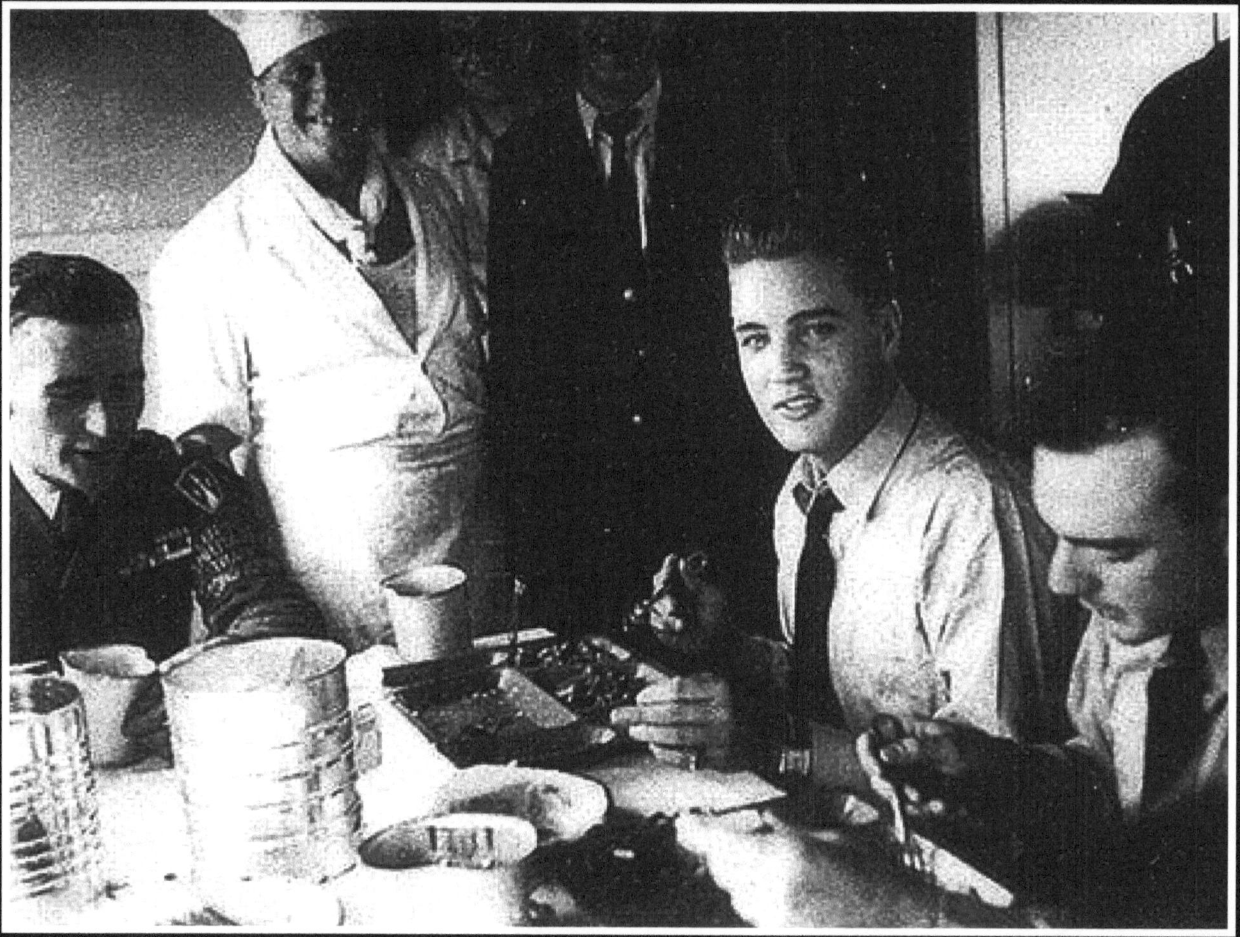

Elvis is dining at the ship's Captains table.

On November 18, 1958, the interviews and press conference were released on an extended play entitled *Elvis Sails*. It reached #2 on the EP charts. It was released in several countries as shown in the next two pages.

Side 1: Press Interview with Elvis Presley at Brooklyn Army Terminal, September 22, 1958.
Side 2: Elvis Presley's Newsreel Interview with Pat Hernon in the Library of the U.S.S. Randall at sailing time.

A small hole was punched in the top of the back cover so that the fans could hang it on a wall. Presumably another brilliant marketing idea from Elvis' manager.

ELVIS' 1959 CALENDAR

Photos courtesy of All Star Shows
© RCA

EPA-4325

JANUARY
Elvis' Birthday January 8, 1935
First Million-seller Recorded (Heartbreak Hotel) January 10, 1956
First National TV Appearance January 28, 1956

FEBRUARY

MARCH
Elvis Inducted into the Armed Services
March 24, 1958

APRIL
Elvis Bought Home for Family in Memphis
April 10, 1956

MAY

JUNE
Elvis Graduated from Humes High School, Memphis
June 1953

JULY
Elvis' Biggest Selling Record Recorded
DON'T BE CRUEL
b/w
HOUND DOG
July 2, 1956

AUGUST

SEPTEMBER
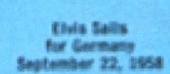
Elvis Sails for Germany
September 22, 1958

OCTOBER

NOVEMBER
Elvis' Extended Play Album Sales Passed 5,000,000
November, 1957

DECEMBER

------ Pop EP Albums ------

EXTRA—ELVIS SAILS
The Press Interviews Elvis Presley—
RCA Victor EPA 4325

A natural. Even tho portions of this were aired on TV at the time of the Presley departure for Europe, this should become a collector's item for the fans. On side one is the interview with the general press. Side two has an interview with the newsreel people and then in the library of the ship which took him to Germany Pat Hernon gets a final word from the singer. It was all very dramatic. A great gift item.

Japan, January 1959

England, 1960

Japan, May 1959.

Spain, 1959. The *Elvis Sails* cover was used, but contained four songs" "Paralysed", "Long Tall Sally", "First In Line" amd "When My Blue Moon Turnes To Gold Again."

Picture, number 1 of 300, taken and signed by A. Wertheimer.

Acknowledgments

I am thankful to the Elvis fan clubs all over the world, particularly their websites which were an invaluable resource. A few were consulted regularly, such as www.nowdigthismagazine.co.uk, www.elvisinfonet.com, www.elvispresleymusic.com.au, www.elvis-collectors.com, www.elvisechoesofthepast.com, www.elvispresleyphotos.com. Facebook sites such as the ones from Sanja Meegin and Tanja Graf are an endless source of rare pictures.

Many thanks to Paul E. Peters who, as he puts it, is making sure Elvis pictures are seen in their correct angle.

I would be remiss if I did not mention all the help I got from the Web, particularly Wikipedia, the free Encyclopedia. It has become an unfailing source of information. Conversely, the information available on the internet is regurgitated so many times that it is extremely difficult to trace the original source of the material, too often at the expense of the originator.

In addition to the sources mentioned above, most pictures are either from private collections or appeared on internet sites such as Pinterest, Tumblr, Sly Mino and others. Every effort has been made to trace the copyright holders, but it has not always proved feasible. I do however extend our thanks to anyone we may not have been able to contact, and should a specific credit be required, it will appear in any further edition of this book.

I thank my wife Dorothy for her continuous and insightful help during the years of researching and writing this book. Her expertise and recommendations have made this book much better than I had first imagined it.

Websites

The following websites have been consulted.

www.nowdigthismagazine.co.uk
www.elvis-collectors.com
www.pinterest.com/slymino
www.elvisanddenise.tumblr.com/archive
www.vinceveretts.tumblr.com/tags
www.elviscentrum.p2a.pl
www.elvislightedcan.free-forums.org
www.elvisconcerts.com
www.scottymoore.net
www.facebook.com. elvis presley fan club luxembourg
www.elvicities.com
www.706unionavenue.nl
www.freeforumzone.com
www.50sspirit.blogspot.com
www.ourdailyelvis.wordpress.com
www.fyeahelvispresley.tumblr.com
www.elvis-history-blog.com
www.elvis-foreveryone.com
www.keithflynn.com
www.elvisblog.net
www.thewonderofelvis.tumblr.com
www.elvis100percent.com
www.clintreno.tumblr.com
www.elvispresley.ru
www.crowdfunding-bad-nauheim.de
www.elvisstuff.co.uk
www.elvis-express.com
www.elvisdaily.com
www.elvisromania.ro
www.buzzjack.com
www.kaywheeler.com
www.rockabillyhall.com
www.elv75.blogspot.com
www.50plus-treff.de/forum/elvis-fans
www.elvispresleyindex.com.br
www.elviscollector.info
www.memphisflash.de
www.elvis-tkc.com

Bibliography

The following magazines and books listed are the ones that deal with only one theme and are connected with his music or a particularly important period of his life. In other words, books that cover his entire career, or books that deal with his relationships with people, such as his manager or some girlfriends or again exploitative ones are not considered.

Elvis Files Magazine
Published by Erik Lorentzen
www.elvisfiles.no

All magazines and books published by Erik are a must for Elvis fans.

ELVIS, The Man and His Music
Published by Trevor Cajiao.
https://www.nowdigthismagazine.co.uk

This magazine is a must for hardcore purist fans.

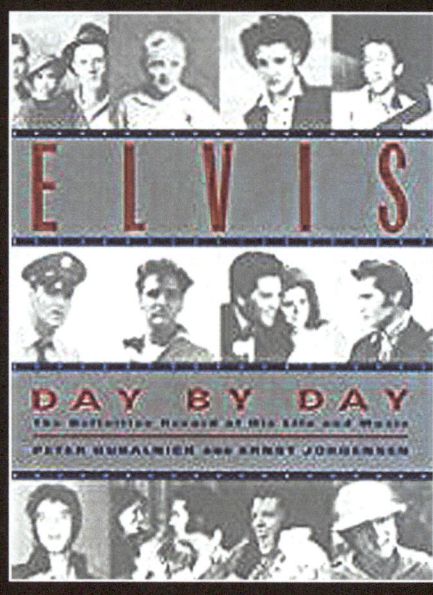

Elvis, Day by Day
Peter Guralnick, Ernst Jorgensen
Ballantine Books, New York
Copyright date: 1999

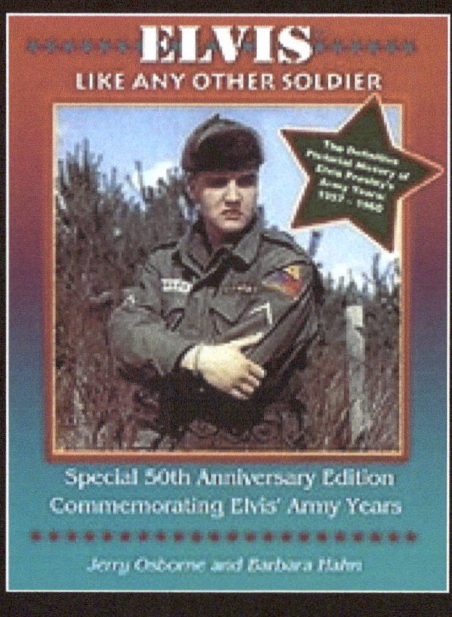

Elvis Like Any Other Soldier
Jerry Osborne, Barbara Hahn
Osborne Entreprises Publishing
Copyright date: 2010

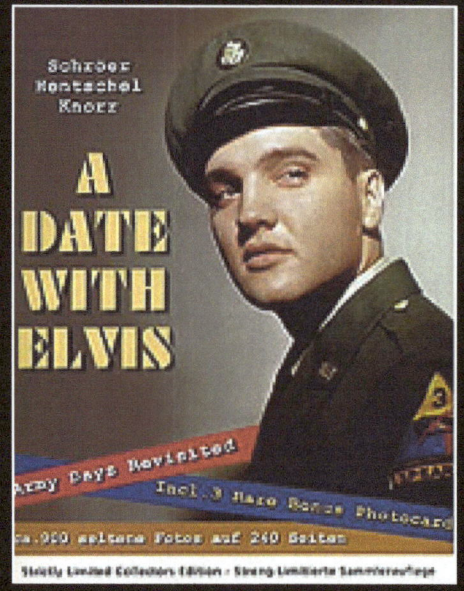

A Date With Elvis
A. Schroer, M. Hentschel, O. Knorr
Epik Verlag
Copyright date: 2011, second edition

Private Presley
Andreas Schroer
William Morrow
Copyright date: 1993

www.ingramcontent.com/pod-product-compliance
Lightning Source LLC
Chambersburg PA
CBHW040904020526
44114CB00037B/52